Shakespeare's Garter Plays

Shakespeare's Garter Plays

Edward III to *Merry Wives of Windsor*

Giorgio Melchiori

DELAWARE

Newark: University of Delaware Press
London and Toronto: Associated University Presses

Associated University Presses
440 Forsgate Drive
Cranbury, NJ 08512

Associated University Presses
25 Sicilian Avenue
London WC1A 2QH, England

Associated University Presses
P.O. Box 338, Port Credit
Mississauga, Ontario
Canada L5G 4L8

The paper used in this publication meets the requirements
of the American National Standard for Permanence of Paper
for Printed Library Materials Z39.48-1984.

Library of Congress Cataloging-in-Publication Data

Melchiori, Giorgio.
　　Shakespeare's garter plays : Edward III to Merry wives of Windsor
/ Giorgio Melchiori.
　　　　p.　　cm.
　　Includes bibliographical references and index.
　　ISBN 0-87413-518-4
　　1. Shakespeare, William, 1564–1616—Knowledge—History.
　2. Literature and history—Great Britain—History—16th century.
　3. Historical drama, English—History and criticism.
　4. Shakespeare, William, 1564–1616—Histories.　5. Falstaff, John,
Sir (Fictitious character)　6. Order of the Garter—In literature.
　7. Kings and rulers in literature.　8. Nobility in literature.
　9. Honor in literature.　I. Title.
PR3014.M45　1994
822.3'3—dc20　　　　　　　　　　　　　　　　　　　93-48123
　　　　　　　　　　　　　　　　　　　　　　　　　　　CIP

In memory of Philip Brockbank (1923–89)
and for Doreen

Contents

Acknowledgments

The first chapter of part 1 of this book reproduces with many changes and additions the British Academy annual Shakespeare Lecture for 1986, published as "The Corridors of History: Shakespeare the Re-Maker," *PBA* 72 (1986): 67–85. The second chapter is based on the paper "Reconstructing the ur-*Henry IV*," contributed to *Essays in Honour of Kristian Smidt,* ed. P. Bilton et al. (Oslo, 1986), 59–78. The last two sections of chapter 3 develop and correct in many ways the contents of two short notes that appeared in periodicals: "The role of Jealousy: restoring the Q reading of *2 Henry IV,* Induction, 16" (*SQ* 34 [1983]: 327–30), and "Dying of a Sweat: Falstaff and Oldcastle" (*N&Q* ns 34 [1987]: 210–11). The first chapter of part 2 incorporates some suggestions contained in a paper delivered in Italian at the meeting on "Shakespeare a Verona e nel Veneto" held in July 1986, published in *Atti e Memorie dell'Accademia di Agricoltura Scienze e Lettere di Verona* 6/37 (1987): 291–303. The central section of the second chapter develops ideas previously hinted at in a short note, "Which Falstaff in Windsor?," included in the privately printed album for Kenneth Muir on his eightieth birthday, *KM80* (Liverpool, 1987), 98–100.

Most of part 1 of this book depends on research done when I undertook an edition of *2 Henry IV* for the New Cambridge Shakespeare (published 1989) at the same time as I was engaged with Vittorio Gabrieli in editing for the Revels Plays the most puzzling among Elizabethan histories, *The Book of Sir Thomas More* (*Sir Thomas More. A Play by Anthony Munday and Others,* Revised by Henry Chettle, Thomas Dekker, Thomas Heywood, and William Shakespeare, Manchester University Press, 1990). My debt to the general editors of the two series, Philip Brockbank and Ernst Honigmann respectively, goes well beyond any acknowledgement.

Part 2 owes much to the work done in editing and translating into Italian *Edward III* for inclusion in my bilingual edition of Shakespeare's *Teatro Completo* (Vol. IX: *I Drammi Storici, Tomo Terzo* [Milano: Mondadori, 1991], 215–437). But it was enriched by the further research I am still engaged in, in view of another edition of *Edward III* for the New Cambridge Shakespeare under the general editorship of Brian Gibbons. To Richard Proudfoot I am deeply indebted for the great help he gave me over the editions of *More* and of *Edward III*.

I have mentioned very few of the many who taught me and helped me, not only with their advice and the interest they took in my work, but, what is even more valuable, with their friendship. I must add to their names at least those of Muriel Bradbrook and Stanley Wells, while what I learnt through the years from them and from a number of other scholars has become so much part of myself that I am sure I forgot to acknowledge it in my notes. I apologize to them all for these involuntary appropriations, and for the misrepresentations of their thoughts and findings that may have crept into my text. I am grateful to the unidentified publishers' readers who, by finding a number of faults with earlier versions of the manuscript, forced me to rethink and reshape it, intervening with radical cuts, and at times unplanned additions. The remaining faults are all my own.

It is a pleasure to acknowledge the help received from a number of institutions, especially the University Library and the English Faculty Library in Cambridge, but most of all the president, the fellows and the members of Clare Hall, Cambridge, who, since 1980, have welcomed me and Barbara back year after year—it is there that I thought out and wrote most of this book. The book itself, though, would never have been undertaken without the inspiration, the guidance, the indulgent friendship of Philip Brockbank, in the last years of a dedicated and courageous life; nor could it have been completed without the constant hospitable generosity of Doreen Brockbank. To her, and to his living memory, I dedicate this book.

Introduction

The present study, by providing a new approach to six Shake-spearean plays—mainly Histories—staged in the last years of the sixteenth century, ultimately reveals a "figure in the carpet" woven through them all that is strictly relevant to a reconsideration of the ideological stance of the dramatist. I use deliberately the adjective "Shakespearean" because the admission to the official Shake-speare canon of one of the plays, *The Reign of King Edward the Third,* no doubt a collaborative enterprise, is still meeting with some resistance. The diffidence that has so far relegated this play among the apocrypha, although a late romance like *The Two Noble Kinsmen,* written in collaboration with Fletcher, is now unquestion-ingly included in all editions of the complete works, is due to the fact that collaboration in the Jacobean theater was a limited prac-tice and authorship was regularly acknowledged, so that credits were given to the authors, or at least the main author, on title pages, whereas instead playbooks for the public stage in the early Elizabethan age were, with a few exceptions, the fruit of collective work, and the authors remained anonymous.

The other plays in what, for lack of a better definition I call a Shakespearean sextet, are those that are generally described as the second, or Lancastrian, historical tetralogy, with the addition of the comedy that is naturally associated with them through the figure of Falstaff: *The Merry Wives of Windsor.* A reconsideration of the genesis of the Lancastrian cycle of Histories reveals the deceptiveness of the very notion of tetralogy. A more appropriate description, in view of the way the two Parts of *Henry IV* came to be written, could be the one used by an author of remarkable fantasy fiction, Douglas Adams, for his quartet of *Hitchhiker* nov-els: "a trilogy of four". The idea that Shakespeare conceived his major dramatic cycles of histories as sets of four consecutive plays is, in fact, the result of an a posteriori process of reordering plays that had a different origin. Even the first historical "tetralogy,"

comprising the three Parts of *Henry VI* plus *Richard III*, was originally undertaken and staged, in the opinion of scholars like the
editors of the Oxford *Complete Works*, simply as a two-part play on
the *Contention between the Two Famous Houses of York and Lancaster*
(now Parts Two and Three of *Henry VI*); only some time later
Part One was devised presumably to bridge the gap between a
play or plays already successful on the stage—*The Famous Victories
of Henry the Fifth*, possibly, as Philip Brockbank believed, by Robert
Greene—and the two plays dealing with the war of the Roses.
Richard III came later to round off the Yorkist cycle, replacing
the outdated *True Tragedy of Richard the Third*, which, like *Famous
Victories*, had been produced years before by the Queen's Men.

One of the points of the present study is to replace the notion
of tetralogy with the suggestion that the six plays in question could
rather be seen—but were certainly not conceived or planned—as,
ideologically, a single dramatic structure, whose five acts were each
a separate history play, with the addition of the Falstaff comedy
in the spirit of the final jig that was the customary conclusion of
all shows on the public stage.

The common feature of the sextet is the presence in the plays
of a constant though just perceptible pattern, a Jamesian figure
in the carpet—not a deliberate design or a consciously recurring
theme, but a motive only hinted at, which is gradually revealed as
we trace backward and forward the casual ways the plays came to
be written. The motive is suggested by the ambiguous Shakespearean attitude in these plays toward two basic principles that
can be summarized in the words *Policy* and *Honor*, an attitude
amply explored and debated in recent criticism of his works from
different angles, politics and ideology, gender and genre, histori-
cism and cultural materialism, in what Gary Taylor has recently
attempted to present as the "reinvention" of Shakespeare.

The invisible thread that runs through the implicit presence of
this ambiguity in the plays can be detected, on the one hand, in
the creation of the figure of the anti-hero, Falstaff, in its different
reincarnations in history and comedy, and, on the other, in the
open or covert allusions to the institution—the Order of the Garter—which seemed to figure emblematically in Elizabethan England both Policy and Honor through the rites of Knighthood.
The Garter is, in fact, the figure in the carpet of the Shakespearean sextet.

The reinvention of Shakespeare in our time has entailed extremely illuminating explorations of the social, historical, and ideological, as well as literary background of his time. The angle of approach chosen in the present study is in a way more limited, but, as I hope to show, no less rewarding. The starting point for the whole of the first part is a reconsideration of what, in a pioneering study still valid after sixty years, Muriel Bradbrook called *Elizabethan Stage Conditions,* meaning the strictly theatrical practices affecting the work of actor and playwright in Shakespeare's time. A precious document of some aspects of these practices is the manuscript *Book of Sir Thomas More,* which reveals the influence of the vigilant intervention of various forms of control and censorship, as well as the ways the work of the different collaborators in the preparation of a script, from "plotter" to author, to bookkeeper, took place. The other opportunity is offered by a study of the genesis and growth of the Lancastrian cycle of histories, which, besides throwing further light on censorial interference, is the most thorough and complex demonstration of the frequently overlooked theatrical practice of the "remake" of successful older productions, and of the different stages through which it may pass, from rewriting to the devising of "sequels."

These practices are transformed by the dramatist into the tools of his craft and bear witness to the policy he must adopt in the objective stage conditions in which he operates. In fact, a double level of policy is suggested by the Henry plays: the playwright's policy in taking advantage of current theatrical practices to show the operation of Policy in history, through the figures of the hero, Prince Hal/King Henry V, and of the anti-hero, Falstaff. The first chapter of this book illustrates that what is known as the Lancastrian tetralogy was originally conceived as, at most, a trilogy of remakes of old plays (*Woodstock* for *Richard II* and *The Famous Victories of Henry the Fifth* for *Henry IV* and *Henry V*); an intervention of a censorial nature caused the rewriting of the second of them *(Henry IV),* and commercial reasons suggested the addition of a sequel. But what counts most is the emergence in the remade plays of the basic theme of Policy associated with Power, involving not only the historical or fictional characters and events appearing in them, but even more the author's dramaturgic policy in their presentation. This is made clear in the other two chapters of the first part of the book, devoted, on the one hand, to a detailed conjectural reconstruction of what must have been the structure of the original one-play version of *Henry IV,* where Sir John Old-castle was the name given to the character who was to turn into Falstaff in the rewriting; and, on the other hand, a survey of the far-reaching implications of this transformation, through a close reading of those passages that were not present in the original one-play Oldcastle version of *Henry IV* and represent, therefore, the author's second and final thoughts. What matters at this stage is not so much the Oldcastle/Falstaff tangle, as the centrality of the new Falstaff and especially of his catechism of Honor, which calls into question the values extolled by Elizabethan chivalry. The tangle involved in the creation of the Falstaff anti-heroic figure is the inextricable interrelation of Honor, Policy, and Power. For this reason the second part of the present study is mainly devoted to Falstaff, taking into account his five Shakespearean reincarna-tions: Sir John Fastolf disgartered by Lord Talbot in *1 Henry VI,* Sir John Oldcastle in the one-play version of *Henry IV,* the "abomi-nable misleader of youth" in *1 Henry IV,* the old man rejected by Prince Hal in *2 Henry IV,* and finally the philandering Knight of the Garter Inn in *The Merry Wives of Windsor.*

Particular attention is devoted, at first, to the origin of the Fals-taff prototype, not so much out of the historical Oldcastle (who indeed "is not the man"), but as a theatrical creation, "born" on the stage, as he tells us, "about three of the clock in the afternoon, with a white head, and something a round belly" (*2H4.* 1.2.187–89). Beyond the traditional notions of the Morality Vice and of the Lord of Misrule, his ancestry is traced to a Captain in an English comedy that Anthony Munday had adapted from an Ital-ian original, by a thorough cleansing process that included the transformation of a vulgar inarticulate *bravo* (not even the boastful *Capitano* of Commedia dell'Arte) into a typically English character. The play, *The Two Italian Gentlemen,* which established the model of the romantic comedy on the British stage, was certainly known to Shakespeare, who echoed its title in the first of *his* romantic comedies.

The central chapter of the second part extends the inquiry into the Falstaff figure and the emergence and significance of his name by means of a thorough reconsideration of the relationship between *The Merry Wives* and the court entertainment presumably offered on the occasion of the Garter feast of 23 April 1597. They are seen as two distinct productions, both including Falstaff, but whereas the Falstaff presented in the earlier show derived from the unworthy knight who made a brief appearance in *1 Henry VI,* the Falstaff of the comedy was meant to revive the character who appeared in the Lancastrian histories. This view entails an attempt at reconstructing the nature and general outlines of the 1597 Garter entertainment, as well as at establishing the chronological sequence of composition of all the Falstaff plays, including the Windsor comedy.

The recurrent theme of the Garter and of Shakespeare's attitude to the values it represented leads inevitably back to the collaborative play devoted to the founder of the Order, Edward III. Though in fact the play, surprisingly, does not mention this central event itself in the reign of the king, in its celebration of the values presiding over the education of princes it is as much a "Garter play" as any in the Falstaff cycle, and even more revealing of the dramatist's policy in dealing with so sensitive a subject. The policy failed in respect to the treatment of the Scots, which caused the suppression of *The Reign of King Edward the Third* as the natural prelude to the Lancastrian histories, and its condemnation to anonymity. Ironically, the political *defaillance* (the ironical presentation of the Scottish ancestors of the future King of England James I) occurred in the scenes in which the author was intent on a much subtler exercise of policy: the episode of Edward's infatuation with the Countess of Salisbury, which unexpectedly extends over the whole of the first two acts of the play. Although Froissart and Painter tell the story of the Countess of Salisbury with no reference to the founding of the Order of the Garter, the author knew that Holinshed, who makes no mention of the story, suggests that the legendary garter picked up by the king at a court ball, which caused the foundation of the Order and prompted its motto, was that of the Countess. A moral history based on the interplay of sexuality and power—the theme of so much of Shakespeare's work, from *Lucrece* through *Measure for Measure* to *Cymbeline*—lies at the root of the celebration of the values of honor and nobility in the Order of the Garter. It is by going back to the history of Edward III that we discover the secret thread that links together the Shakespearean saga leading up to the last incarnation of Falstaff, "corrupt, corrupt, and tainted in desire," in royal Windsor.

Shakespeare's Garter Plays

Part 1
The Corridors of History

1

The Corridors of History: Shakespeare the Remaker

Shakespeare contributed to the English stage the most sizable body of plays on the previous three centuries of English history. The editors of the 1623 Folio grouped them together as belonging to a separate dramatic genre from Comedies and Tragedies, and ordered them according to the chronological sequence of the events narrated, though they had been written and performed in a substantially different order. It is a tribute to Shakespeare's skill that they can be seen now as part of an overall design, presenting in ten installments (or rather eleven, taking into account a play excluded from the Folio that shall be discussed later) a consistent picture of those three centuries in the history of England. But the discrepancy between the two chronologies—that of history as such and that of composition and performance of the single plays—should sound a warning: Shakespeare was first and foremost not a historian or a political thinker but a man of the theater, whose genius served the needs of his fellow players, by observing the rules of a trade and responding to the demands of a market.

Show Business: Sequels and Remakes

No doubt, the historical and ideological context in which the histories were conceived is extremely relevant to an exploration in depth of the values they represent. But surely a reconsideration of their strictly theatrical context is no less important when first approaching them. The fact that should never be lost sight of is that Shakespeare was a supreme expert in a trade or a business— the show business—that in many of its essentials has not changed much through the centuries. The most notable change perhaps is in terminology: now there is talk of media and of mass response, and viewers' and listeners' attendance is charted out with sophisticated devices; but in the first Elizabeth's time the only mass media available were the theater and the preacher. A frequent mistake made when drawing parallels between then and now is that of using as a term of reference the present-day stage, whereas the focus should rather be on film and television. The film industry in its early stages was busy creating a stardom system that would appeal to the imagination of audiences who were hardly aware of the names of the actual authors (if they can be so defined), the directors. In the same way, the Theatre and the other London playhouses were built in the 1570s and 1580s to provide entertainment as a money-making proposition. What mattered was the effectiveness of the entertainment provided, the story, the action, and the acting—not the message or the literary quality of the show. Of course, some men of letters joined in, but without claiming authorship: they simply contributed their particular skills in exchange for a fee. The case of private or academic shows, where authorship was generally acknowledged, is different, but our concern is now with public theaters.

It took quite a while before popular audiences began to value the names of some theater poets as a guarantee of a good afternoon's entertainment: the title pages of plays that got into print counted on the names of the companies that acted them rather than on those of the authors. Shakespeare is a case in point: *Titus Andronicus, Romeo and Juliet, Richard III*, and even the First Part of *Henry IV* appeared anonymously, and we have to wait till 1598 to see his name on the title page of a play. The parallel is once again with the cinema, where the text of the show is a script in which a number of people have a hand (or at least a main finger, as Thomas Heywood was to say about his contribution to the stage[1]), and that is further modified during the "shooting." Henslowe's diary from 1597 to 1603 hardly ever records a payment to a single author for a play. Playscripts, or "books," for the public stage were considered the result of collaborative endeavors, although apparently the practice petered out at the turn of the century, and possibly somewhat earlier in the case of the Chamberlain's Men. In one respect the parallel with the cinema does not hold: whereas the film, once made, is permanently recorded and remains unchanged (except for possible censorial intervention, manipulation by distributors, or damage to the copy), the play changes with each individual performance, so that the printed text of a Shakespeare play, as Stanley Wells so beautifully put it, is merely "the snapshot that got taken"[2] among the numberless ones that remain unrecorded.

Two common practices in the film industry deserve particular attention because they were foreshadowed in Elizabethan show business. The best known is that of the sequel or follow-up: when a film has been particularly successful, the same firm and team of actors and scriptwriters devise new and frequently preposterous adventures for the popular hero, Tarzan or Frankenstein, Rocky or Rambo—a practice that has nothing to do with radio or television serials, such as "The Archers", "Coronation Street", "Dallas", or the innumerable and literally endless tele-novelas: these develop from the serial novels of the last century. The sequels instead were certainly practiced by the Elizabethans: there would have been no *Death of Robert Earl of Huntington* (Munday's and Chettle's play on Robin Hood) if his *Downfall*, produced a year before, had been a flop.

The second and less noted practice is that of the remake: when a film has been successful, after a few years a rival company produces a new version of the same subject—especially if drawn from a novel or from history—with a completely different cast and director, possibly a new slant to the story, and it is hoped improved technical devices. This is exactly what happened in the Elizabethan or Jacobean theater, where the rivalry between companies was as fierce as that in the modern film world; and it must be granted that Shakespeare was the greatest expert in remakes for the Chamberlain's/King's Men. It is known for certain that at least three major plays of Shakespeare were new treatments of subjects that had been successful on the stage before, when acted by the Admiral's or the Queen's Men. The "ur-*Hamlet*" is unfortunately lost, of the Admiral's *Troilus* there remains only a leaf of the plot, and probably the much earlier *True Chronicle History of King Leir* would never have gotten into print if Shakespeare had not produced his masterly remake of it. Unlike the common run of current film remakes, Shakespeare's are not just forms of revamping past successes; he went back to the sources of the earlier versions and recast the stories his own way, leaving the treatments presented by the rival companies far behind.

The great Shakespearean remakes, *Hamlet, Troilus and Cressida,* and *Lear,* belong to the first five years of the new century; but the greatness of those achievements is implicit evidence that Shakespeare had acquired his skill as a remaker at an earlier stage. It can be said that he was led to it in the first place by the popularity of the history or chronicle play on the public stage in the late eighties and throughout the nineties of the sixteenth century. I shall not enter into such different but equally controversial questions as those of the much debated relationship between the Second and Third Parts of *Henry VI* and *The Contention between the Two Famous Houses of York and Lancaster,* or between *Richard III* and the earlier anonymous *True Tragedy.* David Bevington points out[3] that theatrical censorship became much more sensitive to topical references of a political nature from 1593 onward, and Janet Clare discovers the earliest evidence of censorial intervention in such plays as *Doctor Faustus, Sir Thomas More, The life and death of Jack Straw, The First Part of the Contention (2 Henry VI)* and *Woodstock,* all written or printed between 1592 and 1594.[4] The feeling of unrest in the country induced the Master of the Revels to put an end to the tolerance that in previous years had permitted the emergence of what I would call "alternative histories", that is, plays for the public theater criticizing the abuses of authority and underlining the rights of the common people. I believe that Shakespeare's first remakes are to be seen within this context, which is better defined in theatrical rather than in strictly political terms.

The Role of Censorship: *Sir Thomas More*

Touching on the subject of censorship, the obvious starting point must be *The Book of Sir Thomas More,* a manuscript play in the hand of Anthony Munday[5] with a number of additions in five different hands, one of which (hand D) has been identified as Shakespeare's. I offer, at this point, some of the conclusions arrived at when recently editing the play in collaboration with Vittorio Gabrieli.[6] In the first place, far from being an accumulation of stylistically discontinuous fragments (as most modern editors maintain), *Sir Thomas More,* once all the additions are put in their proper places, is one of the best constructed plays of the age. It is a coherent whole, dramatically effective: the authors of the additions show a fine sensitivity to the needs of the stage, the smooth sequence of different scenes within a framework represented by the traditional pattern of the *De casibus virorum illustrium*, the fall of the great. None of the additions is a gratuitous interpolation; most of them act instead as dramatic links tightening up the overall theatrical structure. But there is one inconsistency, not on the theatrical, but more precisely on the ideological level. In the original version of the play in the hand of Anthony Munday the London citizens involved in the xenophobic riots of Ill May Day 1517 are shown as justified in their resentment, which has nothing to do with racial hatred. The behavior of John Lincoln, the leader of the popular rebellion against the insolent strangers, is nothing short of noble, or even heroic, in his last speech from the scaffold before his execution:

> Then to you all that come to viewe mine end,
> I must confesse, I had no ill intent,
> but against such as wronged vs ouer much.
> And now I can perceiue, it was not fit,
> that priuate men should carue out their redresse,
> which way they list, no, learne it now by me
> obedience is the best in eche degree.
> And asking mercie meekely of my King,
> I paciently submit me to the lawe.
> But God forgiue them that were cause of it.
>
> (*619–28)

Lincoln's death parallels very closely that of More at the end of the play:

> I confesse his maiestie hath bin euer good to me, and my offence to his highnesse, makes me of a state pleader, a stage player, (though I am olde, and haue a bad voyce) to act this last Sceane of my tragedie. (†1931–34)

In a much earlier scene Surrey and the other noblemen had justified the citizens' resentment against what is described in Holinshed as "the insolent sawcinesse" and "the diuelish malice" of the aliens, offending "against all honestie, equitie, and conscience" (*Hol.* 3.840).[7]

The arguments against the strangers put forward by Lincoln

in the famous addition in hand D are of a completely different nature and tone:

> ... He that will not see a red hearing at a harry grote, butter at a levenpence a pounde meale at nyne shillings a Bushell and Beeff at fower nobles a stone lyst to me
>
> (Add.II.123–25)

> ... our Countrie is a great eating Country, argo they eate more in our Countrey then they do in their owne
>
> (Add. II.127–28)

> ... they bring in straing rootes, which is meerly to the vndoing of poor prentizes for whats a sorry p[ar]snyp to a good hart
>
> (Add.II.130–31)

This is the language of Jack Cade and his followers in the *Second Part of Henry VI:* the rightly indignant citizens of the earlier scenes, who later, when sentenced to death, are ready to face it with dignity and even a touch of humor, become in the hand D addition an irresponsible rabble in the hands of a clownish demagogue.

Now, from the moment it was suggested that hand D was Shakespeare's (and I share this opinion), attention and praise concentrated on these three additional pages, and the rest of the play was at best disregarded, because it did not fit in with the Shakespearean fragment. In other words, the paradoxical view was taken that the whole should suit the part, instead of the other way round. But the reasons for this unfitness, this ideological contradiction, become clear if the *More* fragment is properly seen as an early instance of Shakespeare rewriting—not remaking, but the one process is a first step in the direction of the other—a scene written originally by somebody else. It is not a question of the poorer literary or dramatic quality of Shakespeare's addition, or of its interrupting the flow of the action; on the contrary, the passage in hand D is, from this point of view, superior to the lost scene that it replaces: it handles beautifully the rhetoric of persuasion, and it is a masterly treatment of a crowd scene. But it does not belong to the context created by the original author of *More:* this is a different crowd from the one presented in the previous scenes. The Elizabethan historical context of the Shakespearean addition[8] may help to get into focus More's admirable speech, which is perfectly structured by dovetailing two main arguments. The transformation of forensic oratory into poetry is achieved by placing a forceful restatement of the Tudor doctrine of the sacrality of kingship within the context of Christian compassion for the oppressed. The pathos of More's plea in favor of the strangers is enhanced if we take into account a further topical context: in 1592–93 there was in London a strong reemergence of anti-alien feeling, culminating in the seditious rhyme posted on the wall of the Dutch churchyard on 5 May 1593, of which unfortunately we know only the first four lines:

> You, strangers, that inhabit in this land,
> Note this same writing, do it understand,
> Conceive it well, for safeguard of your lives,
> Your goods, your children, and your dearest wives.[9]

—a threat that was taken so seriously by the Privy Council as to cause the arrest of a number of suspects, among whom was the playwright Thomas Kyd. (A further consequence was the interrogation and indirectly the death of Christopher Marlowe.) The rhyme in the Dutch churchyard ended with an ultimatum to the strangers to leave the country. More's plea, in Shakespeare's fragment,

> ymagin that yo^u see the wretched straingers their babyes at their backs,
> w^t their poor lugage plodding tooth ports and costs for transportation
> (Add.II.197–99)

recalls More's own description of the condition of the evicted tenants in *Utopia*[10] to provide a point-by-point reply to the rhyme. The reaction of the crowd to the speech, "letts do as we may be doon by" (a Christian proverb from the Sermon on the Mount), is exactly the same as the decisive argument with which on 23 March 1593 Henry Finch obtained the rejection in the House of Commons of a bill against the aliens in London.[11] It reflects the view of the authorities on the question of the strangers in 1593, which I believe is when Shakespeare wrote his addition.[12] It is reasonable to suggest, therefore, that the rewriting of the scene, replacing what must have been in the original version a more sympathetic presentation of the case for the May Day rebels, was motivated by the events of the time. This is not tantamount to accusing Shakespeare of being a time server: the theater in the Elizabethan age was the nearest equivalent to the modern mass media, entailing a certain caution in those who work for them, as well as a very different conception of political issues.

Shakespeare as Remaker

Some of the reasons obtaining in the rewriting of one scene of *Sir Thomas More* must have been at work also in the early Shakespearean remakes of popular history plays. But, significantly, at least in two instances, even the remade plays got into some sort of the same trouble. Such is the case of *Richard II*, which was undoubtedly intended to counteract the utterly negative presentation of the figure of the king in the titleless anonymous manuscript play, variously known as *Woodstock*, or *The First Part of Richard II*.[13] To call Shakespeare's play a remake is perhaps stretching a point: what can be said is that it was originally conceived as such—as a rival stage presentation of Richard's reign—but the determination to stress the other aspect of the king's figure, his role as victim extenuating his abuses as a morally weak ruler, forced the playwright to focus on later developments in Richard's reign. Paradoxically the intention of presenting the king in a more favorable though still ambiguous light, although resulting in an extraordinary artistic and dramatic achievement, involved further problems of a political nature, as is shown by the omission of the deposition scene in the first three editions of the play and by much more serious trouble later, when its performance on the eve of the Essex rebellion caused the imprisonment of members of the Chamberlain's Men.

Commercial reasons are instead predominant in the decision to remake a long-standing success of the rival company of the Queen's Men, a company that by the midnineties was in a phase of rapid decline. *The Famous Victories of Henry the Fifth* had held the stage triumphantly in the eighties as, among other things, a vehicle for the popular clown Richard Tarlton, who died in 1588.[14] Unfortunately the *Famous Victories* that went into print in 1598—probably because of the success of a Shakespearean play on the subject—is a much reduced and wretchedly reported text of a play that originally must have been in two parts.[15] The Chamberlain's Men's idea was to remake the original *Victories,* known to them at least through performances, into two plays: one, *Henry IV,* mainly concerned with the youthful private misdemeanors and thorough reformation of Prince Hal, the other, *Henry V,* dealing with the famous victories proper, without forgetting to make the audience merry with Katherine of France.

Let us consider the first of these two plays, planned as the company's history for the year 1596 in the same way as *Richard II* had been the history for 1595. To avoid confusion with the later extant version in two parts, I shall call it the ur-*Henry IV.* The obvious approach was to preserve the general outline of the previous play, describing the pranks of the prince and his companions that were surely responsible for the earlier popularity of the *Famous Victories,* but to turn it into a proper history by injecting into the new version large sections derived from Holinshed's and Stowe's chronicles that should provide the supporting framework. The delicate point was the behavior of the Prince at the beginning of *Famous Victories,* presented as the personal promoter of such abuses as that of robbing his father's receivers and intimidating them into silence. Three ways were found to attenuate this negative impression. The first and most far reaching was the creation out of history and legend of a counterpart to the Prince among the rebels—the impulsive and heroic Hotspur, over whom the Prince was to triumph in the end, showing that he was the better man; no historical or other source attributes to the Prince the actual killing of Hotspur. A second more direct way was not to let the Prince be a robber in his own person: he pretends to organize the robberies, but, in fact, he merely robs the robbers and returns the booty to the rightful owners. Third, the main responsibility for the Prince's (attenuated) misbehavior was attributed to a more mature "Councellor of youthfull sinne."[16] *Famous Victories* had called the most authoritative of the knights who seconded the Prince in his enterprises Sir John Oldcastle, familiarly Jockey, although he was also the most moderate among them. Oldcastle, therefore, became the misleader of youth in Shakespeare's remake of the play. Shakespeare would be the readier to accept the name for this new creation of his if he had been influenced at some time by the attitude of the English Roman Catholics toward the historical Oldcastle Lord Cobham, in contrast with his celebration first by Bishop John Bale[17] and later by John Foxe as a Protestant protomartyr. This opens up a very controversial field of speculation, which I shall touch on only briefly. Ernst Honigmann has pointed out the youthful Shakespeare's connection with eminent Lancashire Catholic families,[18] and it is significant that the typical interjections of the Hostess in *2 Henry IV* are reminiscent of, and to be found only in, the language attributed to Lady More by Sir Thomas More's great biographer, Nicholas Harpsfield, in a forbidden book widely circulated in manuscript (eight copies are still extant) in recusant households.[19] It is worth noticing that Harpsfield had published in Antwerp in 1566 those Latin *Dialogues* (another book treasured by recusants) containing a virulent attack against Oldcastle as a pseudomartyr, which Foxe furiously refuted in page after folio page of his *Acts and Monuments*.[20] It has been suggested that Shakespeare created the character of Oldcastle as a bitter satire of the Lollards and Puritans in general, and that the Prince's words in *1 Henry IV*, 2.2.80–81,[21] "Oldcastle sweats to death, And lards the lean earth as he walks along" are a callous allusion to the terrible execution of Oldcastle by fire.[22]

But Shakespeare's first and foremost preoccupation in remaking the first part of *Famous Victories* was no doubt that of producing as entertaining a play for the London audience as possible, as well as providing a much stronger historical background to the events, and at the same time, extenuating the Prince's misbehavior by shifting responsibility for it on to a new comic character. In *Famous Victories* the task of providing rough and ready clowning was entrusted to Derrick the Carrier, whereas Shakespeare transferred it to one of the knights: I am inclined to believe that Will Kemp took originally the role of scarlet-nosed Rossill, the nickname of Sir John Russell (playing on the Italian for "red": *rosso*), who was later to become Bardolph,[23] while Oldcastle, developed into a major comic and not clownish part, was taken by an actor with a much wider range than that of the professional clown.[24]

My conclusion is that the History acted in 1596 by the Chamberlain's Men was Shakespeare's remake as *Henry IV* of the first part of the *Famous Victories*, centering on the figure of the Prince, of his outsize evil angel, Oldcastle, and of his mirror image, Hotspur, acting as his involuntary good angel. The idea that *Henry IV* was originally not only conceived, but also actually performed on the stage as a single play, was advocated most forcibly nearly half a century ago by John Dover Wilson.[25] Since then, though, it has lost some of its credit. This is surely due in some measure to the habit of looking at Shakespeare's histories as grouped into tetralogies, a sound and helpful notion in the terms Tillyard presented it,[26] but seriously misleading if understood as implying that Shakespeare actually planned in advance to produce sequences of four plays as organic units. If, to underline the consistency of the historical sequence, we must speak in terms of tetralogies, let me suggest that the second of them was meant to include *Edward III* (a play written not long before 1595, which Richard Proudfoot[27] has convincingly claimed as part of the Shakespeare canon), *Richard II, Henry IV,* and *Henry V.* One concern of the present book is to indicate how and why things turned out differently, so that we can perhaps detect, with all due discrimination, a sextet rather than a tetralogy of plays covering a century of English history, from the 1330s to the 1420s.

The History of Henry the Fourth

Nobody doubts that there must have existed an earlier version of the *Henry IV* play or plays with Oldcastle instead of Falstaff, but the latest proposal is simply to replace, in Part One of the Shakespeare text, the name of Falstaff with that of Oldcastle. Editors who do not follow this injunction, we are told, "join defenders of the corrupt and derivative Vulgate, against the reforms of Erasmus."[28] I am afraid I must be classed with the defenders of the Vulgate, not because I do not believe that in many instances it would be enough to substitute one name for the other to get to what Shakespeare originally wrote—I have just done so myself when, in quoting a well-known line from act 2 scene 2, I restored Oldcastle's name for the present unmetrical "Away, good Ned: Falstaff sweats to death."[29] What Kristian Smidt has called the "unconformities"[30] that are scattered in large numbers through both Parts of *Henry IV* bear witness to a process of adaptation, rewriting, and especially amplification of materials originally organized in a much tighter and more economic dramatic structure. My next chapter attempts a reconstruction of this original structure, the ur-*Henry IV*, that is to say, Shakespeare's one-play version of the history, featuring Oldcastle, Harvey, and Rossill instead of Falstaff, Peto, and Bardolph respectively, as well as the episode of the box on the ear of the Lord Chief Justice, but ignoring completely the second rebellion in the North and the Gaultree episode and many sections of the comic scenes in the first and practically all those in the second Part of the plays as we have them now.

Details of the metamorphosis undergone by the original one-play version are discussed later:[31] what must be immediately stressed is that such a play could not have been presented on the stage at a more unfortunate time. Henry Carey, first Lord Hunsdon, the Lord Chamberlain and patron of Shakespeare's company, died on 22 July 1596, and although the company remained under the patronage of his son George Carey, second Lord Hunsdon, the office of Lord Chamberlain was transferred to William Brooke, Lord Cobham. It was a short-lived transfer, because the Lord Cobham died in March 1597, and the office was then returned to the younger Carey, so that the company was able to resume the name of Chamberlain's Men; but these few months were enough for the Lord Cobham, as supervisor of all public entertainment, to be shocked by the success of a play featuring his martyred ancestor Sir John Oldcastle as its main comic attraction (although surely his part was by no means as extended as that of Falstaff in the later versions). The company, temporarily known as Lord Hunsdon's Men, was forced to withdraw the play just after discovering the formidable appeal of the newly created character of the fat misleader of youth. To throw away altogether such a promising script would have been a sorry waste. The obvious solution was to produce, as the History for the next season 1597, a reelaboration of the same play on Henry IV, removing from it the offending presentation of the Protestant martyr, but not the character himself; on the contrary, Falstaff, now no longer identified with Oldcastle, the historical Lord Cobham, should be given ampler scope to delight the London audience: the tavern scenes (now *1 Henry IV*, 2.4 and 3.3) were much extended, and his portrait was rounded off with the introduction, at the crucial point of the battle that was to mark the Prince's utter reformation and transformation, of Falstaff's catechism on honor (5.1.127–41).[32]

Leaving aside for the time being the reasons for the choice of the name of Falstaff to replace that of Oldcastle,[33] what should be noted is that the expansion of Falstaff's role entailed the problem of his relationship with the Prince. In remaking the first part of *Famous Victories,* Shakespeare had attenuated the direct responsibility of the Prince, in line with the picture presented toward the end of *Richard II* (5.3) by Bolingbroke, inquiring about his "unthrifty son," "with unrestrained loose companions. . . . Which he, young wanton and effeminate boy, Takes on the point of honour to support So dissolute a crew" (*R2*, 5.3.1, 7, 10–11). The ur-*Henry IV* was the story told in unambiguous terms of this wanton boy, who, out of a misguided sense of loyalty to loose companions, had gone so far as to box the Lord Chief Justice on the ear; exactly that episode—his acceptance of being sent to prison—marked the young man's awakening to a sense of personal responsibility, the beginning of his reformation, of that crescendo that gave him heroic stature at Shrewsbury, leading to his coronation and the rejection of his "dissolute crew." In the rewriting of the remake the greater space allowed to Falstaff as an obvious box office draw entailed the risk of enrolling the Prince too firmly on his side, diminishing the credibility of an unprepared revulsion from wanton ways. The solution was to show from the beginning the Prince's awareness of his difference from Falstaff and his companions by underlining that his living as Falstaff's shadow and sharing his language and attitudes was mere pretense—hence the introduction of the well-known soliloquy at the end of the first scene in which the Prince appears (now *1 Henry IV*, 1.2. 204–26):

> I know you all, and will awhile uphold
> The unyoked humour of your idleness, . . .
> I'll so offend, to make offence a skill,
> Redeeming time when men least think I will.

After this self-revelation the scene with the Lord Chief Justice would be out of character, as being appropriate to a misguided boy, not to one intent on redeeming time; so it must go and be replaced with an action more in keeping with such premises.

As Harold Jenkins brilliantly surmised,[34] at some point in the writing—or rather rewriting—of the new act 4, Shakespeare must have realized that all the additional material concerning Falstaff and the Prince could not fit into a single play. There would be no room for the last scenes of the ur-*Henry IV* such as the death of the king and the rejection of Oldcastle/Falstaff. These scenes, therefore, were set aside for possible use, and the play was planned as culminating in the battle of Shrewsbury, leaving no doubts as to the transformation of the Prince into the victorious Henry V—

as well as to the retribution of the "irregular humourists." The latter objective was achieved by a masterly device that only a professional man of the theater could have thought of. Taking a hint from *Famous Victories*, where the episode of the box on the ear of the Lord Chief Justice is immediately followed by its comic reenactment by Derrick the Clown and his partner John Cobbler, in the new *Henry IV* the suppressed scene with the Justice was replaced with what is known as the play-acting scene (2.4.378–481), where the Prince, impersonating his father, condemns "that villainous abominable misleader of youth, Faltstaff," and, when Falstaff, impersonating the Prince, pleads "Banish not him thy Harry's company—banish plump Jack and banish all the world," replies in his own person as well as the king's: "I do, I will."

A Sequel to a Remake

In other words, *1 Henry IV* was written, or rewritten, in 1597, as a self-sufficient play with an open ending. So, if it did not meet with success on the stage, some of the scenes left over from the ur-*Henry IV* could be conflated into the opening scene of *Henry V*, the remake of the second part of *Famous Victories*—after all, in *Famous Victories* the rejection of the Prince's companions, the archbishop's arguments for the English rights to the French crown, the episode of the tennis balls with the declaration of war, and the confirmation in office of the Lord Chief Justice were all rolled into one single scene.[35] If the rewritten play was instead successful, all the material left over and much more could be incorporated in a straight sequel to it. Significantly, when Part One of *Henry IV* was first published in 1598 it bore the title *The History of Henrie the Fourth*, with no indication that it was a "First Part," suggesting that, when *1 Henry IV* was completed and first performed in 1597, Part Two had not yet been planned—it was at most thought of as an open option.

The exceptional number of Quarto editions of *1 Henry IV* shows how well the first Falstaff play was received: the option must be taken, the history for the 1598 season must be a sequel to *Henry IV*. The task was not easy: what was left over from the ur-*Henry IV* could fill at most one act with historical material and a couple of scenes with comedy. The only chance of reinforcing the historical side was to turn once again to Holinshed and include the second rebellion and the unsavory Gaultree episode—an awkward decision, because, in the hurried replacement of offending names in ur-*Henry IV,* Shakespeare had picked on that of Bardolph for Russell,[36] but now he could not avoid introducing a duplication, because the historical Lord Bardolph had played a major role in the second rebellion. On the other hand, the best way of strengthening the comic scenes was the creation of a host of new characters as well as extending the parts of those who had already appeared: here are Pistol, Doll Tearsheet, Justice Shallow and Justice Silence—allusive names that could figure well in a moral interlude. It is significant that Part Two should be introduced by Rumour "painted full of tongues," the only case (apart from Time in *The Winter's Tale*) in which Shakespeare presents on the stage an allegorical personification. Part Two acquires, for better or worse, a new dimension: not History but a revisitation of known events in the key of moral allegory, so that when Falstaff enters it is easy to recognize him as the morality Vice. And, as Lionel Knights pointed out,[37] the play in its final form is run through by the theme of time, of man's subjection to time and physical decay, so macroscopically presented in the figure of Falstaff—a different Falstaff from that of Part One, as the Lord Chief Justice remarks (*2 Henry IV,* 1.2.178–86):

> Do you set down your name in the scroll of youth, that are written down old with all the characters of age? Have you not a moist eye, a dry hand, a yellow cheek, a white beard, a decreasing leg, an increasing belly? Is not your voice broken, your wind short, your chin double, your wit single, and every part about you blasted with antiquity? and will you yet call yourself young? Fie, fie, fie, Sir John!

Knights recognizes that "the tone of *Henry IV Part II* is entirely different from the tone of detached observation of the earlier plays," it is "markedly a transitional play. It looks back to the Sonnets, and the earlier history plays, and it looks forward to the great tragedies."[38]

This is true, although the obvious morality element in the earlier group of Histories lacked the new complexities of the later one. They offered themselves in fact as mere chronicles, culminating in the monstrous apparition of Richard Crookback, duly defeated by that mirror of knighthood, Richmond, the founder of the Tudor dynasty bringing about—as the historian Edward Hall put it—the union of the two noble and illustrious families of Lancaster and York. History was approached single-mindedly as the record of events full of sound and fury, leading toward one great goal, not—as that misleading historian and schoolmaster, Mr Deasy in Joyce's *Ulysses*,[39] was to put it—the manifestation of God, but at least, in Edward Hall's words, the triumph of peace, profit, comfort, and joy in the realm of England.[40]

Let me put it this way: Shakespeare's occasional collaboration in a play like *Sir Thomas More*, presenting a problematic view of recent history, awakened, or reinforced, his awareness that such a simple conception of the historical process would not hold. Then there came the remakes, partly motivated—like his contribution to *More*—by the wish, or the necessity, of taking into due consideration the sensitivity of the censor regarding the presentation of the negative side of authority, particularly royalty. *Richard II* is a case in point: in reacting to the negative view of Richard in *Woodstock*, Shakespeare had to alter the focus of history itself, no longer the conflict between the powers of good and those of evil represented in two opposing factions, but a conflict inborn in human nature itself. Richard is a contradictory personality to be explored per se.

The Role of Policy: Prince Hal to Iago

No less contradictory is Richard's successor, Henry IV, at one and the same time a wise and rightful ruler with a noble mission, and a guilt-ridden usurper. *Famous Victories* shirked the problem by leaving the king in the shadow, but in the remake, where he had the title role, it was solved by feats of eloquence, like the soliloquy, now in Part Two, 3.1, "How many thousand of my poorest subjects," paralleling the magnificent oratory of More in Shakespeare's contribution to the earlier play. The most remarkable development, though, is one I have already mentioned: the introduction, in the rewriting of the ur-*Henry IV* as Part One, of the Prince's self-revealing soliloquy right at the beginning of the play (1.2.206–12):

> Yet herein will I imitate the sun
> Who doth permit the base contagious clouds

> To smother up his beauty from the world,
> That when he please again to be himself
> Being wanted, he may be more wondered at
> By breaking through the foul and ugly mists
> Of vapours that did seem to strangle him.

The historical prince, in contrast with the tavern-hunting wanton and effeminate boy (*and* with the impulsive and outspoken Hotspur), follows a deliberate policy. His character is ambivalent, but deliberately so, whereas the inner conflicts of Richard II and Henry IV were presented as part of their natures. Hal is from the beginning the political man—not necessarily the Machiavellian, the deceiver for deception's sake, but rather the statesman who calculates the impact of his behavior in respect of the interests of the institutions. What emerges here is the relationship between history and politics, a problem that had not been faced at all in the early Histories, where the motives of the action were represented by naked thirst for power and conquest, the generous pursuit of national ideals, or the most villainous forms of plotting and counterplotting. Like T. S. Eliot's Gerontion, Shakespeare has now realized that

> History has many cunning passages, contrived corridors
> And issues, deceives with whispering ambitions,
> Guides us by vanities[41]

The realization that policy—a word generally used with negative or at most ironical connotations[42]—could be an instrument in the pursuit of noble ends, conditions both Parts of *Henry IV* on the stylistic level as well. From the unified language of *Richard II,* based on the principles of the highest rhetoric, we move to a constant alternation of high and low, a see-saw that in Part Two becomes unbalanced; in fact, the relationship between the Prince and Falstaff is completely changed, or rather it hardly exists. The only time—apart from the final scene—they are together, in the tavern at Eastcheap (2.4), the Prince appears in another traditionally political role: that of the disguised ruler spying on the actions of his subjects. After which Falstaff becomes a recruiting officer in the provinces (3.2)—surely a role transferred from the earlier part of the history, where it belongs[43]—and this time he recruits soldiers for a war that does not take place because of the "policy" of Prince John of Lancaster, who entraps the rebels at Gaultree with false promises. Part Two is the triumph of policy: the last meeting of the Prince, now King Henry V, with Falstaff—the rejection scene—is in fact no meeting at all: Henry has become a personification of kingship, hardly acknowledging the existence of his former companion: "I know thee not old man."

The king comes fully into his own of course in *Henry V*, which was the History performed by the Chamberlain's Men in the 1599 season. There is no mistaking the dominant figure in this History: apart from those of Hamlet, Richard III, and Iago, that of King Henry is the longest part that Shakespeare ever wrote for one of his characters, 8,338 words according to Marvin Spevack's *Concordance*,[44] nearly one third of all the words spoken in this long play. History, in it, is physically present in the frequent interventions of the Chorus—the positive side of Rumour in *2 Henry IV*. Without Falstaff, without the English background of tavern, inn, or village life, the comic unhistorical scenes in the play create a new dramatic genre, which could be called "comedy of language," or rather "languages," with the four captains, Fluellen, Gower, Macmorris, and Jamy and their marked national accents and features, and with the French, from the boastful Dauphin to Princess Katherine, already singled out as a source of merriment in the Epilogue to the previous History. The part of King Henry himself is constantly played on two distinct linguistic registers: the noble oratory of the great verse speeches, based on ample rhetorical patterns of immediate appeal (the proper use of rhetoric is to produce consensus), and, on the other hand, the subtle dialectical prose speeches, ironical and unashamed of sophistry—a sophistry apparent not only in the wooing of Katherine, but even more in the night scene before Agincourt (4.1), in which, once again, Henry takes over the role of the disguised ruler.

What emerges from the stylistic duality of Henry's part is not his humanity but the portrait of a statesman, of the *homo politicus*.[45] The relation between the two registers used in Henry's speeches is, according to Spevack's *Concordance*, roughly sixty-nine percent verse to thirty-one percent prose. It is interesting to ascertain which other leading characters in Shakespeare's plays have a similar ratio between verse and prose, since the proportion of prose to verse is a revealing, because it is unconscious, criterion in the construction of character. Later English histories cannot be taken as terms of reference: after *Henry V* Shakespeare wrote none (apart from the collaborative and much later *Henry VIII*). Perhaps the fact itself (Shakespeare forsaking the writing of histories) is intrinsically significant: we should ask ourselves whether it was due to a decline of the genre in contemporary theater,[46] or rather to Shakespeare's new consciousness of the primacy of the exploration of the individual character and the motives of human behavior over the chronicling of events. His last history play, *Henry V*, had yielded him the character of the politician, ambiguous even when pursuing noble ends. The nearest thing to an English history play after *Henry V* is *Macbeth*, which in fact Tillyard included in his treatment of Shakespeare's histories; one wonders whether Macbeth's statement that life "is a tale told by an idiot, full of sound and fury, signifying nothing" represents the author's ultimate view of history.

According to the statistical data, for what they are worth, in Spevack's exhaustive *Concordance*, after Hamlet, and apart from Macbeth (who speaks only in verse) and Timon (whose linguistic register is constant to the point of monotony), there are only two other characters who dominate the plays in which they appear as much as Henry V by speaking over thirty percent of the words used. The first is the Duke in *Measure for Measure*—the *deus ex machina* in a sinister story, a ruler in disguise with a vengeance. The fundamental ambiguity of his role is borne out by that of his language, alternating the high sententiousness of his moralizing speeches in verse with plotting and planning—apparently all for the best—in prose: and the proportion between the two registers is very close to that which we find in Henry: 69.4 percent verse, 30.6 percent prose. Stepping out of history into fiction, the politician follows more devious ways: the disguised ruler pursues justice through the deceit of the bed-trick and the pretense of a capital execution—through many cunning passages and contrived corridors.

At this point it is perhaps no surprise to find that nearly the same proportion between verse and prose (seventy-one percent to twenty-nine percent) obtains in another character who, like Henry, speaks over thirty-two percent of the words in the play where he appears, although not in the title role: Iago in *Othello*. There is some variation within the registers of his language, the subject of masterly studies such as those of Madeleine Doran or Alessandro

Serpieri:[47] sophistry, the rhetoric of negation, reticence and suspension, affect his verse—and especially his extended soliloquies—as much as his prose, and the latter is at times degraded to the coarseness of barrack language. But the outer balance is the same: the variation is in degree, not in kind. Freed from the fetters of history, the politician reveals a deeper layer of ambiguity: "I am not what I am."

The parable is complete: from the wanton Prince Hal transformed into the victorious Henry V, through the Duke of dark corners in Vienna, to the "ancient" in the Venetian army. Is this the inevitable progress of the politician? I prefer to think that this is the lesson of history. Three hundred years later, Mr Deasy's statement in *Ulysses* that "History moves to one great goal, the manifestation of God" was countered by young Stephen Dedalus with: "History is a nightmare from which I am trying to awake." This was written in 1916, and Eliot's "Gerontion" at about the same time: it had taken Eliot and Joyce the experience of the First World War to discover the deception of history. Shakespeare learned the lesson as a man of the theater should: by *remaking* history—turning its deception into dramatic ambiguity, which is the true life of a play.

2

Reconstructing the Ur-*Henry IV*

It is time to provide chapter and verse for the broad assumptions already put forward about the genesis of the "Henry" plays and their relationship with the much earlier *The Famous Victories of Henry the fifth,* a play we unfortunately know only in a badly reported and reduced version published in 1598.[1] Assuming that the latter was originally in two parts, it is most likely that Shakespeare had planned his remake of them for his fellow actors as two plays, to be called *Henry IV* and *Henry V* respectively. But things turned out differently, and the first of these, *Henry IV,* is now known to us in the form of two plays, though Shakespeare had at first written and presented it on the stage as a single play, now lost (ur-*Henry IV*),[2] in which the character of the "misleader of youth" was called Sir John Oldcastle instead of Falstaff, and two of his companions called Rossill and Harvey instead of Bardolph and Peto. The situation can be summarized in the following terms:

a) The ur-*Henry IV* (1596), now lost, was a remake of the first part of *Famous Victories* (i.e., scenes i–ix).

b) *Henry IV Part One* (1597) is a reworking of ur-*Henry IV,* roughly corresponding to *Famous Victories* i–vii, and was intended as a self-sufficient play with an open ending looking forward to *Henry V.*

c) *Henry IV Part Two* (1598) is a sequel to *1 Henry IV,* incorporating some left-over materials from ur-*Henry IV* previously intended for the early scenes of *Henry V.*

d) *Henry V* (1599) is again a remake of the second part of *Famous Victories* (scenes ix–xx).

Unconformities in *2 Henry IV*

Our starting point for an enquiry into the structure of the lost—or rather, transformed—one-play version of *Henry IV* to reconstruct its main lines is the reconsideration of some notorious incongruities in the Quarto text (1600) not of the First but of *The Second part of Henrie the fourth,* a particularly authoritative text, universally acknowledged to be based, unlike the First Part, on Shakespeare's own foul papers.[3]

Here are the five major *cruces*:

1. The residence of Justice Shallow: Gloucestershire is mentioned only late in *2H4* (4.3.82 and 128), and in the Folio text of *Merry Wives of Windsor* (1.1.4); the location of the famous enrollment scene where Shallow makes his first appearance (*2H4,* 3.2) could well be intended as somewhere on the Great North Road, between London and York.
2. The presence in one play of two characters with practically the same name: red-nosed "Corporal" Bardolph, who already in Part One was Falstaff's closest associate, and the historical Lord Bardolph, appearing in Part Two for the first and only time, out of the pages of Holinshed's *Chronicles.*
3. The speech heading *Vmfr.* (for "Umfrevile") at *2H4,* 1.1.161 (sig. B1).
4. The speech heading *Old.* (for "Oldcastle") at *2H4,* 1.2.120 (sig. B2v).
5. The entrance direction *Enter the Prince, Poynes, sir John Russel, with other* at *2H4,* 2.2.0 (sig. C3v).

The five problems must be treated separately.

1. Shallow-land.—Devoting several pages of his book[4] to the question of Gloucestershire as the residence of Justice Shallow, Kristian Smidt confutes those who try to justify Falstaff's long detour through that county in his northbound journey to York as evidence of his unreliability in military as in other matters and argues that the enrollment scene "must undoubtedly have been designed as part of a single Henry IV play and could only belong to the Shrewsbury plot." In fact, attempts at condensing the two Parts into one either omit the scene altogether—as in the earliest such compilation by Sir Edward Dering in 1623[5]—or place it before *1H4*, 4.2, where Falstaff, on his way to Shrewsbury, does not dare to march his recruits through Coventry because they are "such pitiful rascals," "exceeding poore and bare, too beggerly"; actually, during the battle we learn what happened to his company of scarecrows:

> I haue led my rag of Muffins where they are pepperd, theres not three of my 150. left aliue, and they are for the townes ende, to beg during life. (*1H4*, 5.3.35–38; sig. K1v)

Instead, there is no mention of Falstaff being accompanied by a "charge of foot" in the Gaultree campaign in Part Two. Granting that the enrollment scene had been conceived in view of the Shrewsbury battle now in Part One, which would have led Falstaff through Gloucestershire, how can we explain that no mention of that county has survived when the scene was removed to Part Two? If this is the result of careful revision, it is the more surprising to find, later in the same Part Two (4.3), Falstaff, after the capture of Colevile at Gaultree, asking Prince John "My Lord, I beseech you giue me leaue to go through Glostershire" (4.3.81–82; sig.H1), and announcing at the end of the scene: "ile through Glostershire, and there will visit M. Robert Shallow Esquire" (4.3.128–29; sig. H1v).

Also in Part Two, 5.1, a scene that cannot conceivably derive from ur-*Henry IV,* all local references are to places in Gloucestershire and in the neighboring Warwickshire, and in *Merry Wives* "Robert Shallow Esquire" is said by his cousin to be "in the County of Glocester, Iustice of Peace and Coram."[6] I believe the enrollment scene in Part Two to be a much enlarged reworking of a very short episode in ur-*Henry IV,* which was, in turn, suggested by scene x of *Famous Victories,* where a Captain presses into the army for service in France Derick the Clown and John Cobbler. The episode in ur-*Henry IV* was meant as no more than a comic interlude, in which Shakespeare had introduced the figure of a corrupt country justice of the peace (I doubt that he had already given him the name of Shallow) in contrast with the incorruptible Lord Chief Justice who appeared in earlier and later scenes. Only odd lines of the enrollment episode in ur-*Henry IV* were echoed in *2 Henry IV,* 3.2, but enough to create the confusion in the number of recruits offered and enrolled.[7] Probably the recruitment in the one-play version was merely the opening section of what is now the Coventry scene in Part One, 4.2. This seems confirmed by looking at the "parent" scene in *Famous Victories:* there the Captain manages to press for service not only the Clown and John Cobbler—who tries to evade the call by using arguments very close to those of Mouldy in *2 Henry IV,* 3.2.111–15 and 229–32—but also the thief, causing the Clown's reaction:

> Marry I haue brought two shirts with me,
> And I would carry one of them home again,
> For I am sure heele steale it from me,
> He is such a filching fellow. (*FV,* sig. E1)

Surely this is echoed in *1 Henry IV,* 4.2.42–47 (sig. H3) when Falstaff at Coventry comments:

> theres not a shert and a halfe in all my companie and the halfe shert is two napkins tackt togither, . . . and the shert to say the trueth stolne from my host at S. Albones, or the red-nosed Inkeeper of Davintry.

Ur-*Henry IV,* then, included a scene in which Oldcastle and another "knight" (Rossill/Sir John Russell, who was to become corporal Bardolph, see sections 2 and 5 of this chapter below) were helped by a dishonest country Justice, on their way through Gloucestershire to Shrewsbury, to press some poor devils for the "charge of foot" procured by the Prince for Oldcastle (see *1 Henry IV,* 3.3.186); after the Justice's exit, Oldcastle commented to the knight in terms very similar, if not identical, with Falstaff's at Coventry in *1 Henry IV,* 4.2.1–48. When rewriting the play after the name changes, Shakespeare decided that there was room only for the comment, rather than the actual enrollment scene. Next year, though, looking for material to "bombast" the sequel to the new *Henry IV,* he turned again to the rejected section of the scene in ur-*Henry IV* and, in rewriting it, he not only extended it very considerably through the strong characterization of the recruits and the addition of Justice Silence as a comic partner for the totally recast character of the country Justice, but also, aware of the rerouting of Falstaff's expedition, he carefully avoided any reference to Gloucestershire. The mention of Stamford fair[8] at *2H4,* 3.2.38 looks like a precise attempt at relocating the scene.

But, in the hurry to complete the play, this was soon forgotten: the newly devised Colevile episode (*2H4*, 4.3) was no more than the exact duplication of Falstaff's (originally Oldcastle's) boasting over Hotspur at Shrewsbury, so that the author went back to thinking in terms of the ur-*Henry IV*, where the enrollment took place in Gloucestershire. The request to go through Gloucestershire on his way back (*2H4*, 4.2.82) may well have belonged, in ur-*Henry IV*, to the aftermath of the Battle of Shrewsbury. It was omitted in the rewriting of it as Part One, 5.4, but was revived for Part Two. In fact, the exchanges between Falstaff, Prince Hal, and Prince John in *1 Henry IV*, 5.4.130–58 (sig. K4), ending with Hal's "For my part, if a lie may do thee grace, Ile guild it with the happiest terms I haue," parallel so closely those between Falstaff and Prince John in *2 Henry IV*, 4.3.26–70, 81–85 (sig. H1), ending with John's "Fare you wel Falstaff, I, in my condition, Shal better speake of you then you deserue," that they seem modeled on and adapted from a single scene in ur-*Henry IV*; a surmise strengthened by the well-grounded suspicion that, in the second instance, "Fare you wel Falstaff" is merely a "correction" of the original "Farewell Oldcastle."[9] Here is the reason why, starting from this scene in *2 Henry IV*, Shakespeare went back to thinking of Gloucestershire as Shallow's residence.

2. The Two Bardolphs.—The duplication of Bardolph in Part Two entails a double order of problems: the general question of Shakespeare's naming unhistorical characters in his plays, and the specific case of renaming characters that had appeared in ur-*Henry IV*.

In *Famous Victories* the Prince's companions are repeatedly honored in stage directions with the title of "knights," though in the speeches they are familiarly called by their first names or nicknames: Ned, Tom, and Jockey—the latter being the nickname of Sir John Oldcastle.[10] Together with the "knights," also a professional thief enjoys the Prince's protection, though acting as a freelancer in his robberies; indicated mostly as "Thief" in speech headings and stage directions, his full name—Cutbert Cutter—is revealed only when he is questioned by the Lord Chief Justice (scene iv, sig. B2v), but before that Derick the Clown, robbed by him at Gad's Hill, recognizing him in the street, had called out (*FV*, scene ii, sig. A4v):

> Whoope hollo, now Gads Hill, knowest thou me?
> *Theef.* I know thee for an Asse.
> *Der.* And I know thee for a taking fellow,
>   Vpon Gads Hill in *Kent:*
>   A bots light vpon ye.

In remaking *Famous Victories* into ur-*Henry IV,* Shakespeare adopted the nickname Gadshill used by the Clown for the thief, turning the latter into the low-class "setter"[11] (i.e., the man employed by robbers to spy on their intended victims) for the Prince's knight-companions, whose number he increased from three to four. Falstaff's punning reference to "vs that are squiers of the nights bodie" (*1H4,* 1.2.24; sig. A3v) is surely a fossil of the early version in ur-*Henry IV,* as much as the famous "my old lad of the castle" a few lines later (41-2; sig. A4), referring to the knight's name before the change into Falstaff.

In the remake of *Famous Victories,* Shakespeare had to assign to each of the "knights" good English family names. Sir John Oldcastle was already in the parent play; to Ned he added a surname of old Norman stock, Pointz, turning him into the Prince's confidant;[12] Tom was split into two, as we learn from Poins himself later in the same scene when, planning the Gad's Hill coup, he says, according to the Quarto version (*1H4,* 1.2.162–63; sig. B1): "Falstaffe, Haruey, Rossill, and Gadshill, shal rob those men that we haue already way-laid." What happened is clear: Shakespeare, reusing an odd leaf from ur-*Henry IV,* had carefully "corrected" Oldcastle into Falstaff in headings, directions, and even the body of speeches, but overlooked the other two companions, mentioned here for the first time and for whom he had perhaps not yet devised new names.

In other words, in ur-*Henry IV* those two "knights" had been given names of titled English families, the Harveys and the Russells. The reason for the choice of the two names has been discussed at length by Alice-Lyle Scoufos, who detects in it, as in the case of Oldcastle, a deliberate satirical intention. With regard to Harvey, she is fairly convincing.[13] Sir William Harvey, a gentleman who was knighted in June 1596 (when Shakespeare was remaking *Famous Victories* into *Henry IV*) for services rendered in the Cadiz expedition, was apparently at the time intent on courting the considerably older, widowed mother of the Earl of Southampton, Shakespeare's private patron. His mother's new relationship (that seems to have been legitimized in 1599) must have disturbed the young Earl, only heir of the family fortunes, and he may have been pleased to see Harvey pilloried on the stage as an unscrupulous fortune hunter. Scoufos's reasons for the choice of "Sir John Russell" (the family name of the Earls of Bedford) are much more elaborate, having to do with the Chamberlain's Men's resentment at being prevented from leasing the new Blackfriars theater by the widow of John Russell in November 1596. Apart from the late date, I feel that the explanation given in the discussion of the surviving stage direction "sir Iohn Russel" in section 5 of this chapter is much more direct. What should be noted is that, for Russell, Shakespeare also invented a familiar nickname, Rossill, that offered ample scope for playing with the Italian *rosso* for "red": the "red hill" was to be the main feature characterizing this particular knight—a formidable red nose casting its purple hue on the rest of his complexion. We must concentrate rather on what happened when, for the reasons already indicated, Shakespeare recast ur-*Henry IV* as the new history play for 1597.

In the case of Oldcastle, the offending family name was changed, by a complex process that is fully explored in the second part of this book, into that of a nobleman of ill repute, that Fastolfe or Falstaff covered with shame in *The First Part of Henry the Sixth*,[14] without diminution in his rank but with a considerable increase in the extent of his role. The other three were degraded from knights to commoners. There was no need to rename Ned Pointz, or Poins, because he was presented in a comparatively favorable light. Harvey had a minor role, enough to make up a foursome on occasion, without distinguishing features: he was given the insulting soubriquet of "Peto" that the court gallants in the audience would recognize as the Italian for "fart." Instead, changing the name of Russell/Rossill entailed the loss of the punning reference to the main feature of the character; as a compensation, he must be given a somewhat impressive "historical" name, in ironic contrast with his appearance. When borrowing massively from Holinshed's *Chronicles*[15] to provide a solid historical background to his remake of *Famous Victories*, Shakespeare decided to ignore altogether the central section of the history of the reign of Henry IV, covering the years 1405–1413; many of those pages (525–34) dealt with the second rebellion in the North, culminating in the Gaultree episode and the battle of Bramham Moor. It was in those pages, and only there, that a Lord Bardolph, the closest associate of Northumberland in the rebellion, played a major role—but he had been given no part in ur-*Henry IV*. Bardolph, deprived of his Lordship, seemed high sounding enough as the name of Falstaff's red-nosed partner, so it replaced the offending Russell/Rossill.

When, owing to the success of the rewritten play in 1597, it was decided to give it a sequel—Part Two—Shakespeare was forced to have recourse to the historical matter he had deliberately left out of his ur-*Henry IV,* and the introduction of the historical Lord Bardolph was inevitable. To distinguish him from the "irregular humourist" who had already appeared in Part One, Shakespeare presented the new Bardolph as a kind of incarnation of the misleading allegorical figure of Rumour, whom he had cast as the "Presenter" of the sequel. As Shaaber neatly put it, "Falstaff's Bardolph was too droll a scoundrel to be discarded and truth to Holinshed forbade the omission of Northumberland's ally"[16].

3. Umfrevile.—There is no reason to believe, as has been suggested in view of the survival in the 1600 Quarto of Part Two of the speech heading *Vmfr.* in sig. B1 (1.1.161), that Shakespeare thought at first of avoiding the Bardolph duplication by renaming "sir John Umfrevile" the historical Lord Bardolph, and later changed his mind. A thorough reexamination of the problem[17] has satisfied me that the prefix *Vmfr.* was introduced by an incompetent reviser to fill a gap in the speech headings: running his eye over the previous pages of the manuscript, he found "sir Iohn Vmfreuile" mentioned by the servant Travers at 1.1.34 (sig. A3) and took him to be an interlocutor in the scene. Actually, the casual mention of an Umfrevile in a speech confirms Shakespeare's practice in choosing names that must sound "historical" for odd invented characters. To fill the historical gaps in Part Two, Shakespeare had to restudy that section of Holinshed (pp. 525–34) that he had ignored in ur-*Henry IV.* It is precisely on p. 529/2/34–51, where the "forrest of Galtree" is first mentioned, that we are told that, among the forces that "made forward against the rebels," there were "those who were appointed to attend on the said Lord Iohn [of Lancaster] to defend the borders against the Scots, as the lord Henrie Fitzhugh, the lord Rafe Eeuers, the lord Robert Vmfreuill, & others." Later, dealing with events of 1410–12 ignored by Shakespeare, Holinshed devotes no less than two full folio columns to the actions of "sir Robert Vmfreuill vice-admeral of England" and "his nephue yoong Gilbert Vmfreuill earle of Angus" against the Scots, as well as to a mission in aid of the Duke of Bourgogne, in which the two Umfreviles were accompanied by "Thomas earle of Arundell" and "sir Iohn Old-castle lord Cobham" (*Hol.*, 3, 536/2/65–537/2/56). Umfrevile sounded right for a fighting nobleman: the change of the first name from Gilbert or Robert to plain John avoided identification with Holinshed's Umfreviles, who had been involved in quite different actions.

4. Old. for Oldcastle.—The survival, on sig. B2v of the Quarto of Part Two, of the speech heading *Old.* poses a different problem. It has been unsatisfactorily explained as due to the fact that Shakespeare had already also written most of Part Two before he was forced to change Oldcastle's name or to a memory lapse in the writing of it after the name change. Remembering that the 1600 Quarto is based on Shakespeare's own foul papers, the soundest approach to the problem is to inquire into the state of such papers. Authors used paper sparingly at the time, it being mostly imported and relatively expensive. Whenever possible, odd leaves of the early drafts, with all sorts of interlineations and corrections, were incorporated in the version of a play that a dramatist handed to the bookkeeper in charge of preparing the promptbook. This is the case here: Shakespeare's foul papers of Part Two included odd single leaves from the manuscript of ur-*Henry IV* that the author had discarded when rewriting it as Part One. In other words, act 1 scene 2 of Part Two, though mostly newly written, incorporates a leaf from ur-*Henry IV*, containing a dialogue between Oldcastle and the Lord Chief Justice after the battle of Shrewsbury, and this is borne out by a study of the speech headings in the scene. Up to line 91, when talking to his Boy and to the Justice's servant, Falstaff is designated with the speech heading *Iohn* or *sir Iohn* (except once at 1.72, where he is *Falst.*); from the moment he speaks directly with the Justice (lines 92ff.) his speech heading is constantly *Falst.* up to 1.165, with the exception of the odd *Iohn* at 1.103 and *Old.* at 1.120; then, in the last part of the conversation and to the end of the scene, he becomes again *Iohn,* while the Justice, designated up to that moment either *Iust.* or *Iustice,* becomes for his last five speeches, from 1.178 on, either *Lo.* or *Lord.*[18]

The evidence suggests that, whereas the first and last parts of the scene were newly written, for the central section—from 1.92 to ca173— Shakespeare reused an odd page (judging from the pages in hand D in the manuscript of *Sir Thomas More*, the section would fill exactly one side of a leaf in Shakespeare's handwriting) left over from ur-*Henry IV*, systematically replacing in speech headings *Old.* with *Falst.*, but missing out the one in line 120.[19] This accounts also for the confusion at lines 172–73, in the middle of the last speech headed *Falst.* in Quarto at sig. B3v, where there is "as the malice of his age shapes the one not worth a goosbery," instead of "as the malice of this age shapes them, are not worth. . . ." It was at this point that the manuscript page from ur-*Henry IV* ended in midsentence, and the compositor could not interpret properly the corrections made to join it with its continuation on a new leaf, where Shakespeare modified the thread of the speech to introduce the theme of Falstaff's age, not present in the early version. We may conclude that, after the battle of Shrewsbury, there must have been in ur-*Henry IV* a meeting between Oldcastle and the Lord Chief Justice, recalling Oldcastle's past misdeeds and introducing the subject of the king's illness, in preparation for his death and the dismissal of the Prince's companions.

5. Sir John Russell.—The inclusion of *sir Iohn Russel, and other* in the Quarto entrance direction of 2.2 can easily be taken as a case of "ghost characters," of which there are so many examples in texts set from foul papers.[20] They occur when the playwright plans to include in a certain scene a character (generally mentioned in the source he is following at the moment), and then decides against it, but forgets to cross out the name in the head direction. This actually happens no less than three times in *2 Henry IV*, at 1.3 with *Fauconbridge*, at 4.1 with *Bardolfe* (= Lord Bardolph), and at 4.4 with *Kent*, and in each case the name is in the relevant passage of Holinshed. But *sir Iohn Russel* at 2.2 is a different case, connected with the practice I have just mentioned a propos of the survival of the prefix *Old.*: the inclusion in the foul papers of odd leaves directly from the manuscript of ur-*Henry IV*. The odd leaf in question, this time, contained the beginning of a scene showing the Prince surrounded by his "knights," with the exception of Sir John Oldcastle—a scene modeled on scene vi of *Famous Victories* (sig. C1 ff), which surprisingly leads up to the Prince's reformation. I indicate later the position of this scene and its development in ur-*Henry IV.* For the time being, I am content to point out where Shakespeare first found the name of Sir John Russell, and why he adopted it for one of the "knights." The report, in Holinshed's chronicle of the reign of Richard II, of the capture and execution at "Bristow" of Scroope, Bushy, and Green—well known to Shakespeare, who based on it scenes 2 and 3 of act 3 of *Richard II*—closes with the words (*Hol.* 3, 498/2/74–499/1/3): "they were arraigned . . . and found guiltie of treason . . . and foorthwith had their heads smit off. Sir Iohn Russel was also taken there, who feining him selfe to be out of his wits, escaped their hands for a time." The marginal heading at this point is "A politike madness." Shakespeare must have thought that a politic madman would fit very well among the Prince's companions.

A Reconstruction of the ur-*Henry IV*

The inquiry into the most notorious incongruities in the Quarto of Part Two considerably helps our understanding of Shakespeare's way of rewriting and adding a sequel to a discarded play of his own. More could be learned by taking into account some other inconsistencies in both Parts of *Henry IV,* and especially the many unconformities pointed out by Smidt, which imply, as he says, a process not only of expansion, but also, at times, of condensing material in the original version. Smidt is surely right, for instance, when he says that "the omitted matter may have included a scene in which the Lord Chief Justice sends for Falstaff, and another, or the same, in which Prince Hal delivers the famous blow on the Justice's ear"[21]. A thorough discussion of each separate unconformity in the two plays would fill volumes. I attempt instead a reconstruction scene by scene of ur-*Henry IV,* structured as a sequence of twenty episodes alternating historical events closely derived from Holinshed, and the "comic plot" of the Prince and his companions, modeled on the first part of *Famous Victories.*

Scene I. Historical, substantially reproduced in *1H4,* 1.1, possibly with the rearrangements suggested by Smidt (*Unconformities,*

110–11). Sources: *Hol.*, 540/2 (on the Crusade) and 520/1–521/2 (events in Scotland and Wales).

Scene II. Comic, introducing the Prince, Pointz, and Oldcastle. Suggested by *FV*, i–ii. Reused as *1H4*, 1.2.1–194, as proved by the "survivals" discussed in section 2 of this chapter; there was no final soliloquy of the Prince (11.195–217), which was added in the rewriting to introduce the theme of the Prince's "policy."[22]

Scene III. Historical, accounting for the first rebellion, involving also the Archbishop of York. Reproduced in *1H4*, 1.3. Source: *Hol.*, 521/2–522/1.

Scene IV. Comic: the Gad's Hill episode, derived from *FV*, i–ii. Reused with name changes and substantial additions in the first section, as *1H4*, 2.1–2. I have discussed in the previous chapter the evidence provided by the change from "Oldcastle" to "Falstaff" at 2.2.108.[23]

Scene V. Pseudohistorical (Hotspur and Lady Percy, part of the Hotspur legend). Reused in *1H4*, 2.3, but the letter and Hotspur's comments at 11.1–35 must have appeared, if at all, in a shorter form.

Scene VI. Comic, suggested by *FV*, ii, iv and v. The scene began with the Prince and Pointz, exactly like *1H4*, 2.4.1–28, but without any jokes at Francis's expense; then entered Oldcastle, Harvey, and Rossill, and the unmasking took place as in *1H4*, 2.4.113–283, as testified by the survival in the 1598 Quarto of the speech heading *Ross.* at lines 174, 176 and 180 (sig. D4).[24] But the "noble man of court at doore" announced by an anxious Hostess at 1.287 was not the vague "sir Iohn Bracy from your father" that Falstaff goes to meet at this point in *1H4:* the original scene took a completely different turn. Oldcastle did exit, like Falstaff, but simply to avoid meeting the announced "noble man," who, in fact, was the Lord Chief Justice, come to summon him (in *2H4*, 1.2.55–56, at the sight of the Lord Chief Justice the Boy tells Falstaff: "here comes the noble man that committed the prince for striking him about Bardolfe"). The

Justice was accompanied by the robbed Carrier, like the Sheriff looking for Falstaff later in the same scene of *1H4*, announced by the Hostess in suspiciously identical words with those used at the arrival of the "noble man": "O Iesu, my Lord!" (11.486ff, cf 11.284ff). In ur-*Henry IV* the entrance of Justice and Carrier was followed by an exchange at first very similar to that between Prince and Sheriff at 11.506ff; but then, presumably upon the Carrier's recognition of Rossill (= Bardolph) as one of the robbers, it took the same turn as in *FV*, iv, ending with the box on the Justice's ear and the Prince's commitment to prison. This was replaced in the rewriting, for the reasons given in the previous chapter, by the so-called play-acting scene (*1H4*, 2.4.373–481), which, though absent in ur-*Henry IV*, was suggested by *FV*,v.

Scene VII. Historical: the partition of Britain among Mortimer, Glendower, and the Percies. Reused with amplifications in the final part, as *1H4*, 3.1 Source: *Hol.*, 521/2.

Scene VIII. Historical: the reconciliation between King and Prince, based as much on *FV*, vi, as on Holinshed. Reused as *1H4*, 3.2.

Scene IX. Comic: corresponding substantially to *1H4*, 3.3, but much shorter and without mention of Oldcastle/Falstaff having been robbed. It appears to have been limited to the following parts of 3.3.: the initial dialogue between Oldcastle and Rossill (Falstaff and Bardolph), 11.1–51; the entrance of the Prince marching at 1.87; his telling Oldcastle that he has procured him a "charge of foot" (cf 11.174–92); the final section in verse (11.195–206), although the hypermetrical line 196 about sending letters to John of Lancaster and Westmoreland, closely echoed in *2H4*, 1.2.239–41, suggests some kind of manipulation of the earlier text.[25]

Scene X. Historical: the rebels' preparation. Reused as *1H4*, 4.1. Source: *Hol.*, 522/2.

Scene XI. Comic: the enrollment of recruits and their march to Coventry, suggested by *FV*, x. Amply discussed in section 1 of this chapter. Echoes of the first part of the scene are to be found in *2H4*, 3.2, whereas the second part (Oldcastle and Rossill meeting the Prince and Westmoreland) was reused as *1H4*, 4.2.

Scene XII. Historical: the rebel camp at Shrewsbury, based on *Hol.* 522/1–523/1. Reused as *1H4*, 4.3.

Scene XIII. Historical: the Archbishop sends letters to the rebels, from *Hol.*, 522/1/15–63. Reused as *1H4*, 4.4. Some believe that this scene was introduced at a late stage in *1H4* to prepare for the developments in Part Two.[26] But in Histories it is not unusual for leading political figures to appear only once in a play: of the leaders of the rebellion in *1H4*, Northumberland is present only in 1.3, Mortimer and Glendower only in 3.1.

Scene XIV. Historical: Worcester's interview with the King and his false report on Hotspur, from Holinshed, 523/1/62. Reused as *1H4*, 5.1–2, with the addition of a part for Falstaff (5.1.121–41), whose famous soliloquy on honor was not in ur-*Henry IV*.

Scene XV. Pseudohistorical: the battle of Shrewsbury and its aftermath, based on Holinshed, 523/1/63–524/1/26, with the addition of the Hal/Hotspur confrontation suggested by Daniel's *The First Four Books of the Civil Wars* (1595), and of the "comic" intervention of Oldcastle. Substantially reused as *1H4*, 5.3–5; but instead of Falstaff's last speech at 5.4.162–65 there must have been Oldcastle's request to return through Gloucestershire, echoed in *2H4*, 4.3.81–85. See section 1 of this chapter.

Scene XVI. Comic: the interview between Oldcastle and the Lord Chief Justice, prompted by *FV*, iv and vi. Reused as *2H4*, 1.2.92–174 ca, as discussed in section 4 of this chapter. After some more exchanges (possibly echoed in 11.199–206), the scene presumably closed with the arrival of a Messenger (Gower?) for the Lord Chief Justice, and the ensuing dialogue may have left echoes in *2H4*, 2.1.133–35 and 166–95.

Scene XVII. Pseudohistorical: the sick king soliloquizes on his condition and discusses the state of the country (see *FV*, vi, and *Hol.*, 540/2/60–541/1). Reused as *2H4*, 3.1., a scene occupying a separate leaf of the manuscript of ur-*Henry IV*, at first discarded and then recovered at the last moment for inclusion in Part Two. This accounts for its omission from the first issue of the 1600 Quarto of the play.[27]

Scene XVIII. Comic: the Prince speaks with Pointz, Rossill, and possibly Harvey of the king's illness, and is eventually summoned to court (see *FV*, vi). The first page of this scene became, with many corrections, *2H4*, 2.2.1–64ca, see section 5 above. After some more conversation, now lost, came the summons that is echoed, with many changes, in *2H4*, 2.4.354–65.

Scene XIX. Historical: the death of the king, based on *Hol.* 541, and *FV*, viii. Substantially reused, with several additions, as *2H4*, 4.4–5.

Scene XX. Pseudohistorical: the confirmation of the Lord Chief Justice, the rejection of the companions, and the preparation for the French campaign, based altogether on *FV*, ix. The first part of this scene must have been practically identical with *2H4*, 5.2: Warwick, coming straight from the Jerusalem chamber, announced to the Lord Chief Justice the death of the king; he was followed by the other princes and eventually by the new king who confirmed the Justice in his office and called his first parliament. The entrance of Oldcastle, with Rossill and Harvey (obviously not Pistol or Shallow), must have occurred at this point—with no intervening coronation procession—and the rejection must have taken place in the terms reproduced in *2H4*, 5.5.43–72; as in the later version, the play closed with the comments of Prince John and the Justice (11.97–108), who must have remained on stage after the general exit at 1.72.

The New Dimension of *Henry IV*

Some conclusions can be drawn from this highly conjectural reconstruction. First of all, the ur-*Henry IV* must have been a long play, in the region of 3500 lines; not longer, though, than *Richard III*, *Troilus and Cressida*, or *Coriolanus*, not to mention *Hamlet* that totals about 4000. It was mainly, but not all, as suggested by Morgan and Dover Wilson[28], in verse: the comic scenes were in prose, taking up about one third of the whole, a far smaller proportion than in the two-part play we have now—Oldcastle's role was much more subdued than Falstaff's. It was a well-constructed play, alternating historical scenes drawn essentially from Holinshed, with comic scenes suggested by the *Famous Victories*. In the second half of the play there was an ever greater fusion of the two genres in pseudohistorical scenes.[29] Of course, as in all plays, other sources, historical, anecdotal, and literary could be traced, but I have limited myself to those that provided its basic structural framework. It seems also clear that the already mentioned one-play version of *Henry IV* preserved in the Dering manuscript of 1623 does not reflect, as some suggested, the earlier ur-*Henry IV*, but is instead a later compression of the existing two Parts into one.

What really matters is that, with the transformation of ur-*Henry IV* into the two-part play that has reached us, we have lost a well-constructed and dramatically powerful play, but we have gained a view of history in a new dimension, developing to an unprecedented extent the basic themes of time, statesmanship, and especially policy through a much wider range of characterization.

3

From ur-*Henry IV* to Henriad: Rewriting as Subversion

The process of refashioning ur-*Henry IV* into a two-part play, a process that I have described so far in its external and technical aspects, and that was imposed by reasons of theatrical expediency—censorial interventions and box office considerations—has, in fact, much deeper revolutionary implications, affecting not only the two new plays, but also the whole Henriad, including *Henry V*. It marks a new Shakespearean approach to history, breaking with the tradition of the chronicles and tackling much more complex issues than those faced in the earlier group of history plays or even in *Richard II*, where the remake of the earlier play of *Woodstock* resulted mainly in a magnificent exploration in depth of the ambiguities and contradictions in the character of the king himself.

The original one-play Oldcastle version of *Henry IV* was meant to serve a dual purpose: on the one hand, it was a remake of the first part of what had been a very successful play on the stage, *The Famous Victories*, on the other, it was intended as the continuation of the new history cycle begun with *Richard II*. As such it was, like its predecessor, predominantly in verse, highlighting the main historical events of a reign that the historian Edward Hall defined as "unquiet," and, therefore, hardly heroic in itself. Thus, in the wake of *Famous Victories*, it needed to resort to the legend of the youthful trespasses of Prince Hal (albeit extenuating them) to avoid a certain measure of dullness. The irregular humourists (an admirable definition apparently devised by the compiler of a list of "The Actors' Names" intended to fill a page of the 1623 Folio that a printing house miscalculation would have left blank) were few in the ur-*Henry IV* and appeared in no more than a third of the scenes. It was as yet a moderate break with the tradition of

the chronicle play. The real innovation in the form, the unprecedented attribution of the leading role in a history play to a comic
character, did not come with the remaking, but with the forced
rewriting of the playscript.

In the paper that laid the foundations of the "new historicist"
approach to Shakespeare and late Renaissance literature,[1] Stephen Greenblatt pointed out the subversive implications of the
three Henry plays, in respect to the accepted views of the Elizabethan age. Testing the plays against the touchstone of the report
on "the New Found Land of Virginia" by the mathematician
Thomas Harriot, an eminent member of Sir Walter Ralegh's so-
called school of atheism,[2] Greenblatt remarks:

> The first part of *Henry IV* enables us to feel at moments that we are
> like Harriot, surveying a complex new world, testing upon it dark
> thoughts without damaging the order that those thoughts would seem
> to threaten. The second part of *Henry IV* suggests that we are still
> more like the Indians, compelled to pay homage to a system of beliefs
> whose fraudulence somehow only confirms their power, authenticity,
> and truth. The concluding play in the series, *Henry V,* insists that we
> have all along been both coloniser and colonised, king and subject.
> The play deftly registers every nuance of royal hypocrisy, ruthlessness,
> and bad faith, but it does so in the context of a celebration, a collective
> panegyric to "This star of England," the charismatic leader who
> purges the commonwealth of its incorrigibles and forges the martial
> national State.

Though couched in brilliantly paradoxical terms, Greenblatt's
basic argument—the "political" ambiguity of the plays, the new
dimension in the view of history—coincides with that arrived at
by a different route in the discussion of Shakespeare as a remaker
in my first chapter, tracing in them the emergence and progress
of the theme of Policy. It is significant that nearly all the quotations
from the plays used by Greenblatt to bolster up his view of them
as subversive of Renaissance authority, are from those passages
whose absence in Shakespeare's original ur-*Henry IV* I noted before, passages added in the rewriting of the original version with
the name changes in 1597, and, more extensively, in devising its

sequel as a second part the next year. They are, as it were, Shakespeare's second thoughts.

Refashioning *Part One*

Let us recall the most significant of these rethinkings as I have pointed them out in my attempt at reconstructing the earlier Oldcastle version of the play. Three of them are now placed in key positions in *Part One*.

1. *Prince Hal's Soliloquy* (1.2.195–217): *Policy.* I have already commented on the significance of this addition: it marks the entrance of Policy into History, and, in the very act of stating the necessity of policy as an instrument of good government, it confirms that history itself is deceptive, proceeding by what King Henry IV on his deathbed calls "by-paths and indirect crooked ways" (*2H4*.4.5.184). This is made explicit through the sun/cloud imagery that dominates the passage (the sun being the traditional metaphor for the person of the ruler), culminating in the formal closing couplet:

> I'll so offend to make offence a skill,
> Redeeming time when men think least I will.

History is identified with time. The soliloquy introduces in this way the other major theme that governs—together with policy—Shakespeare's new, or in fact subversive, attitude to history. Devouring time becomes a leading motif, with infinite variations, in the Henriad, growing in intensity and pervasiveness as the new plays develop—though it must have been present in a much more subdued form in the ur-*Henry IV*, if it is true that the night scene of the king's illness (now *Part Two* 3.1) was part of it. In reply to the King's speech (45ff):

> O God, that one may read the book of fate,
> And see the revolution of the times
> Make mountains level

Warwick comments (80ff):

> There is a history in all men's lives,
> Figuring the nature of the times deceased,
> The which observed, a man may prophesy
> With a near aim, of the main chance of things
> As yet not come to life, who in their seeds
> And weak beginning lie intreasured.
> Such things become the hatch and brood of time

There is a deliberate ambiguity in Warwick's words:[3] the "times deceased" evoked by each individual man to create his view of history are also inevitably "times diseased." The implications of the wordplay are farreaching. It involves both the nature of "time" and of "history." Time is the progress of the generations of man through disease and death—a classical conception that in Shakespeare had found its most powerful expression in the sonnets. History, in turn, is by no means the splendid record of the great events of the past, but a subjective reading, an imaginative figuration of the diseases of past times.

Against this background, Prince Hal's determination to redeem time acquires a new wealth of meaning. A speech inserted for essentially cautionary reasons (justifying the misbehavior of the paragon of English chivalry) provides Shakespeare with the imaginative stimulus for a radical reinterpretation of history.

2. *The "play-acting scene"* (2.4.373–481): *Falstaff's First Rejection.* The new light in which Prince Hal was presented, thanks to the introduction of his revealing soliloquy early in the play, entailed the abolition of the scene—surely included in ur-*Henry IV*—in which the Lord Chief Justice, as we are told in *Part Two*, 1.2.55–56, "committed the Prince for striking him about Bardolph." The famous episode of the box on the ear of the Justice,[4] representing the authority of the King himself, was incompatible with a Prince who had compared himself to the sun (the king's majesty) "breaking through the foul and ugly mists of vapours that did seem to smother him." Shakespeare's solution is such as only a man utterly committed to the theatrical profession could have devised: he abolishes the scene of the blow, replacing it with a dramatic insert, a play within the play, acting out exactly on a stage upon the stage the promise contained in Prince Hal's earlier soliloquy. At first Falstaff has the role of the King in the mock performance, while Hal is his unredeemed self. But soon the Prince becomes impatient: "Do thou stand for me, and I'll play my father." Falstaff is

"deposed" and the roles are reversed. The Prince, impersonating the King, breaks through the foul and ugly mists that seem to smother him by proclaiming his determination to reject "that villainous abominable misleader of youth," Falstaff, impersonating Hal, the Prince's former self.

The play-acting scene is a stroke of theatrical genius, placed as it is in the center of the play, and prefiguring its final consummation. The theme of policy is developed in strictly theatrical terms: Prince Hal is the author, the director, and the stage manager of the play within the play; his role coincides with the playwright's— Shakespeare's—role. This dramatic insert is in fact a parable—a parable of the policy of playwriting.

3. *Falstaff's Catechism of Honor* (5.1.121–41) *and the Rites of Knighthood*. It is rather surprising to find Falstaff in attendance at the crucial meeting of the King and Princes with Worcester as envoy of the rebels to determine the event of the civil conflict (5.1). In fact, out of 120 lines, Falstaff speaks only one and is promptly silenced by Prince Hal ("Peace, chewet, peace!")—these two very short speeches being the only ones in prose in a sustained verse scene. It is apparent that they are later insertions and that Falstaff (or rather Oldcastle, as he was then called) did not figure in this scene of the ur-*Henry IV*. Why was he introduced in the rewriting? It appears that it was done for the sake of the prose "coda" added to the scene after the exit of all the other characters except Falstaff and Hal; in other words, for the sake of his final speech, a brief soliloquy commenting on the situation, a parallel to the more extended verse soliloquy of Prince Hal added at the end of 1.2.

As the earlier soliloquy was the statement of the Prince's policy, so this is the expression of Falstaff's policy. The exit line of the Prince to Falstaff had been a grim reminder: "Why, thou owest God a death." Falstaff's reaction, as is well known, takes the form of what he himself calls a "catechism," a definition borrowed from liturgy. The implication is that Falstaff is thinking in terms of religion—the lay cult of chivalry promoted by Queen Elizabeth, those "rites of knighthood" punningly referred to by Shakespeare in the opening scene of *Richard II*.[5] Falstaff is ready more than once to claim the "rights of knighthood," if for no other purpose, to cheat Mistress Quickly out of house and home, by repeating his oath, "As I am a gentleman."[6] An oath that Shakespeare himself could have repeated, because just at the time when he was rewriting the play, on 20 October 1596, his father had been granted a coat of arms, with the proud motto *Non sans Droict,* and William could add "Gent." to his name.[7] It is the sort of oath that, in a much more solemn form, the king in an earlier Shakespearean history had pronounced in pursuit of evil ends. In the second and last great seduction scene in *Richard III,* Richard is ready to swear (4.4.366 ff.; 1623 Folio, sig.s5v):

> [*Richard*] Now by my George, my Garter, and my Crowne.
>   *Qu.* [*Elizabeth*] Prophan'd, dishonor'd, and the third vsurpt.
>   *Rich.* I swear
>   *Qu.* By nothing, for this is no Oath:
> Thy George prophan'd, hath lost his Lordly Honor;
> Thy Garter blemish'd, pawn'd his Knightly Vertue;
> Thy Crowne vsurp'd, disgrac'd his Kingly Glory:

Explicit references to the Order of the Garter in Shakespeare's work are few and far between, and they are generally made only for exposing persons unworthy of the Order.[8] But in the act of exposing them, the essential requisites of true chivalry must be stated, as in this case by Queen Elizabeth, the widow of Edward IV: Honour and Knightly Virtue. This "Honour" is the subject of Falstaff's catechism; "honour" is repeated eight times in twelve lines, leading to a semantic analysis of the word itself:

> What is honour? A word. What is in that word honour? What is that honour? Air. A trim reckoning! Who hath it? He that died a' Wednesday. Doth he feel it? No. Doth he hear it? No. 'Tis insensible then? Yea, to the dead. But will it not live with the living? No. Why? Detraction will not suffer it. Therefore I'll none of it, honour is a mere scutcheon. And so ends my catechism.

The conclusion is not just a comic exhibition of the wily arguments of the speaker in justification of his cowardice; it is a bitterly realistic evaluation of the emptiness of the promises implicit in the rituals of Elizabethan chivalry, the immortal fame conferred by death met in the pursuit of honor and knightly virtue. "Detraction"—the vice of Envy, or slander and indifference—will not allow Honour to live with the living, it will blot out the memory of the virtuous deeds of the dead, so that Honour survives merely as a "scutcheon," a heraldic device undecipherable and, therefore, meaningless to posterity.

I suspect that this is one of the many indirect allusions, amounting in fact to challenges, to the values represented by such chivalric institutions as the Order of the Garter in Shakespeare's works, apart from the few overt references such as the one I quoted from *Richard III.* It is not only Falstaff's, but Shakespeare's policy: by attributing to a cowardly character his own potentially subversive views he apparently discredits them, while, endowing that character with a formidable charge of humanity, he makes the audience identify with him.

Refashioning *Part Two*

Pinpointing specific passages added in the writing of the sequel to the 1597 *Henry IV* is practically impossible because, as I believe, most of the text is new, incorporating only a few historical scenes and one or two odd pages from the comic ones in ur-*Henry IV.*[9] What matters is the development, in this wealth of new material, not only of the theme of policy, which with the introduction of the Gaultree episode becomes absolutely predominant, but also of that of time, especially under its aspects of old age and disease. This is done, on the one hand, by giving a new direction and purpose to some scenes that figured in ur-*Henry IV* in a much shorter form, such as Falstaff's meeting with the Lord Chief Justice (1.2) and the enrollment of the recruits (3.2): in both cases all the stress is now put on old age and time's waste; on the other, by creating new emblematic characters—Doll Tearsheet (as Falstaff says, "Peace, good Doll, do not speak like a death's-head"), Justice Shallow and Justice Silence ("And to see how many of my old acquaintance are dead!" "We shall all follow, cousin")—as well as by modifying those already known to the audience: Mistress Quickly, who in the first part (1.2.39–40), and presumably in ur-*Henry IV,* was described as "a most sweet wench," in the second is a gullible old bawd whose delusions of respectability are reflected in her new language; and Falstaff himself, who in the rewriting of *Part One* (2.4. 453) was referred to as "that reverend Vice," has become the type of Old Mortality and the incarnation of Unredeemed Time.

If it is true, as Dover Wilson maintained, that the two parts of
Henry IV taken together are "Shakespeare's great morality play"[10]
(but would not this be true also of the ur-*Henry IV,* which falls so
naturally within the most common of Morality patterns, that of
the Prodigal Son, a favorite subject of Tudor Interludes?),[11] it
must be said that *Part Two* presents a much more complex and
deliberate morality structure, starting from the names given to all
the new characters introduced into it, from Doll Tearsheet, Pistol,
Shallow, and Silence, down to the Sergeants and the Country Soldiers who make only brief appearances. One is reminded of Falstaff's remark to Prince Hal early in *Part One* (1.2.82–83): "I
would to God thou and I knew where a commodity of good names
were to be bought." But the most striking feature connecting the
rewritten play with the Morality tradition is the presence, for the
first time in a Shakespearean history, of an Induction spoken by
an allegorical figure, as well as of a formal Epilogue. They deserve
a much closer look.

Induction: Rumour and the Role of Jealousy. The speaker of the
Induction of the *Second Part of Henry the Fourth* appears in the list
of "Actors' Names" appended to the First Folio edition of the play
as "Rumour, the Presenter." As the only allegorical "character" in
a Shakespearean play, apart from Time in the much later *The
Winter's Tale,* Rumour is perhaps something more than a mere
personification. The unusually punctilious opening stage direction in the Quarto, that requires that he should enter "painted
full of Tongues," is a clear indication that the actor should wear
a painted coat like those traditionally used for the figures of Fame
or Report in pageants, masques, or interludes. A coat that could
be removed quickly upon his exit, so that the actor impersonating
Rumour could reappear a moment later as the character awkwardly named Lord Bardolph, the bringer of false news from
Shrewsbury, the incarnation in the world of history of the notion
itself of rumor. This technique of doubling parts, by which the
audience was made aware that the character entering upon the
stage was the concrete projection of the abstract principle represented by the allegorical figure that the same actor had just been
impersonating, was a common practice in the sixteenth century.[12]

I discussed in the previous chapter the problem created by the
necessity of having to introduce, when writing a sequel to the first
Part of *Henry IV,* the historical Lord Bardolph, when the same

name had already been used for a commoner in the earlier play. It was perhaps to compensate for this and to avoid confusions and misunderstandings that Shakespeare decided to identify unequivocally Lord Bardolph—as distinct from the "irregular humourist" Bardolph—with the abstract figure of Rumour. And he made doubly sure of the identification by echoing, in a speech of Lord Bardolph, some of the very words with which Rumour had introduced himself to the audience in the Induction. When discussing, in the third scene of the play, with the Archbishop of York, Mowbray and Hastings their chances in the rebellion, Lord Bardolph advises them (3.1.22–24):

> in a Theame so bloody fac'd, as this,
> Coniecture, Expectation, and Surmise
> Of Aydes incertaine, should not be admitted.[13]

The near synonyms "surmise" and "conjecture" are found hardly anywhere else in Shakespeare's work, and never in conjunction with each other. But they figure instead prominently in the key passage of the Induction I referred to. A passage that happens to be textually controversial because it presents different readings in the two original editions of the play. The first edition, the Quarto of 1600, which appears to be set mostly from Shakespeare's own foul papers, reads (Ind. 15–16):

> Rumour is a pipe,
> Blowne by surmizes, Iealousies coniectures,

In the next edition, the Folio of 1623, the same lines read:

> *Rumour,* is a Pipe
> Blown by Surmizes, Ielousies, Coniectures:

Until 1980 all modern editions accepted unquestioningly the Folio reading, which sets surmises, jealousies, and conjectures as the three agents of Rumour. In modernizing the spelling most editors confined themselves to the abolition of the capital letters and of the comma after *Rumour*--

> Rumour is a pipe
> Blown by surmises, jealousies, conjectures

—and only some commented on the peculiar use of the word "jealousies," by referring to *OED:* "Jealousy, 5: Suspicion, apprehension of evil; mistrust. Now *dial.*" But already in 1940 Mathias Shaaber, in his New Variorum edition of the play, remarked:

> The reading of Q, omitting the comma, is perfectly intelligible ("blown by surmises, the conjectures of jealousy"), so that it is a little odd that no one has adopted it.[14]

Only in the most recent editions of the play, for Oxford and Cambridge respectively,[15] the Quarto reading has at last been adopted.

The decision depends on the meaning of the lines in question, which deserves further exploration. Rumour, we are told, is not the originator, but the broadcaster—"pipe" would be rendered in modern journalese as "mouthpiece"—of false reports. Line 16 should indicate who blows the pipe, meaning the real source(s) of such deceptive messages. If we accept the Folio's reading and punctuation, we have a list of three sources of equal importance: the Pipe is blown by Surmises, Jealousies, and Conjectures. All these capital letters are explained by the fact that the Folio compositor—or, more probably according to Prosser, the scribe with a passion for "regularizing" who provided the copy—is inordinately fond of capitalization: nearly all the abstract nouns, and a good many of the concrete nouns, in the Folio text of *2 Henry IV* are capitalized. On the other hand, two of the three nouns listed are practically synonyms: any dictionary will define *surmise* as "conjecture, guess," and *conjecture* as "guess, surmise." It is a common rhetorical device to provide a sequel of synonyms to reinforce an argument. But here the middle word sticks out as being definitely not synonymous with the other two, so much so that some editors explain that "jealousies" are not "guesses" but "suspicions, expressions of mistrust"—in other words, "misgivings." "Jealousies" breaks the sequence of synonyms and weakens the rhetorical construction. Besides, guesses and misgivings are themselves the result of false impressions and misapprehensions, not their sources. The image is confused and unsatisfactory.

It we turn instead to the Quarto reading, modernizing the spelling, without tampering with capitalization or punctuation except for the removal of the comma at the end of line 15 (the compositor of Q is prone to close each line with a comma, independently of the sense)--

> Rumour is a pipe
> Blown by surmises, Jealousy's conjectures,

—we find that "conjectures" is not just a synonym; it is part of a clause in apposition to "surmises," with the specific function of clarifying and extending its meaning. The "surmises" that blow Rumour's pipe, we are told, are not independent agents: they are the instruments of Jealousy. The real originator of the false reports broadcast by Rumour is Jealousy, another name for that most obnoxious of the capital sins, Envy—so frequently presented as the chief Vice in Moralities and Interludes. Envy, together with Pride, is at the root of all social upheaval, the source of civil disobedience and open rebellion. Envy is the moving passion of the many-headed multitude, played upon by Jack Cade in *2 Henry VI* and by the Tribunes in *Coriolanus*.

This accounts for the next few lines of Rumour (17–21), where the "pipe" is said to be

> of so easie, and so plaine a stop,
> That the blunt monster, with vncounted heads,
> The still discordant wau'ring multitude,
> Can play vpon it.

No doubt the Quarto reading reflects Shakespeare's meaning and intentions, and there is important objective evidence for this in the way the line is printed: "blowne by surmizes, Iealousies coniectures" with only one word capitalized. It should be noted that the Quarto compositor is at the opposite pole from the Folio compositor in the matter of capitalization. Whereas in the Folio text of *2 Henry IV* a high percentage of common nouns is capitalized, the Quarto uses capitals very sparingly.[16] In the matter of abstract nouns, regularly capitalized by the Folio, the Quarto makes a very nice and precise distinction: they are capitalized *only* when they can be constructed as part of the rhetorical figure of Prosopopoeia, or personification.

This figure is especially prominent in the first scene, the tone having been set by Rumour, who is Prosopopoeia incarnate on the stage, in more than one sense. Let us compare the use of capitals in the Folio and Quarto versions of Northumberland's speech at 1.1.150–60, an outburst of passionate rhetoric dominated by the figure of personification. Here is the Folio:

> Now binde my Browes with Iron, and approach
> The ragged'st houre, that Time and Spite dare bring
> To frowne vpon th'enrag'd Northumberland.
> Let Heauen kisse Earth: now let not Natures hand
> Keepe the wilde Flood confin'd: Let Order dye,
> And let the world no longer be a stage
> To feede Contention in a ling'ring Act:
> But let one spirit of the First-borne *Caine*
> Reigne in all bosomes, that each heart being set
> On bloody Courses, the rude Scene may end,
> And darknesse be the burier of the dead.

Capitals are distributed haphazardly: why Browes, Act, Courses, and not Houre, World, Darknesse? And now the Quarto:

> Now bind my browes with yron, and approach
> The raggedst houre that Time and Spight dare bring,
> To frowne vpon th'inragde Northumberland,
> Let heauen kisse earth, now let not Natures hand
> Keepe the wild floud confind, let Order die,
> And let this world no longer be a stage,
> To feed contention in a lingring act:
> But let one spirite of the first borne Cain
> Raigne in all bosomes, that ech heart being set
> On bloudy courses, the rude sceane may end,
> And darknesse be the burier of the dead.

Only four abstract nouns are capitalized: Time, Spite, Nature, and Order are the four actors in the mental drama that Northumberland is presenting (note the mention of "stage" and "scene") on the subject of the return to the original chaos. Though prosopopoeia is all-pervasive ("Let heaven kiss earth," "the wild flood," "feed contention," "let one spirit reign," "darkness be the burier"), there is a careful and deliberate discrimination; those four (Spite being another aspect of Envy) were familiar as personifications to the audience from a long tradition of morality plays, a tradition continued in the dramas presented on the public stage.

It would be idle to inquire whether it was Shakespeare himself who in his foul papers had capitalized only these words, or whether a singularly intelligent printer or compositor made the decision. In the same way we do not know whether Shakespeare had written "Iealousies" (meaning "Jealousy's") with a capital in line 16 of the Induction, but there is no question that the Quarto compositor had identified in that word the figure of prosopopoeia, and for this reason capitalized it, while using lowercase for "surmizes" and "coniectures." The only other capitalized word in Rumour's speech, apart from the name of Rumour himself (lines, 2, 11, 15, 22, 39) and some proper names,[17] is "War" (line 14) in a context that leaves no doubt as to its being a personification: "Is thought with child by the sterne tyrant Warre."

The Induction to *2 Henry IV,* enacted by an allegorical figure—Prosopopoeia incarnate—is a little drama in itself, in which the other actors are War (the audience is plunged back by Rumour's words directly into the last act of Part One, the battlefield of Shrewsbury), and Jealousy—that is to say, Envy, the originator of all rebellion and civil strife. Rumour is the pipe "Blown by surmises, Jealousy's conjectures". The same words, as we have seen, are used by the incarnation of Rumour in the world of history—Lord Bardolph out of Holinshed's Chronicles—not to deceive his confederates but to warn them against Rumour's deceptions. As a sober politician, he knows that those conjectures and surmises that he himself had spread in his role of Rumour, are merely the result of Jealousy, and must be mistrusted when getting ready for serious action. In fact, the Induction of *2 Henry IV* spoken by Rumour is a statement of "a bloody-faced theme," the basic theme of the "Henriad," that can be summarized in one word: Policy.

Epilogue: Dying of a Sweat—Oldcastle into Falstaff. The Epilogue of *Part Two* is an extraordinary piece of theatrical expediency; or rather three pieces, because it is composed of three sections, apparently written at different times and serving different purposes. The first is an apology for an unfortunate previous performance that had created some trouble of a political nature; the second could be alternative to the first, when the cloud had blown over, to be entrusted to a popular actor introducing the jig with which all shows ended; but the most interesting is the third, obviously an afterthought, with the declared purpose of whetting the audience's expectation for the next installment of the theatrical saga of the House of Lancaster (the author was busy at the time remaking the second part of the *Famous Victories* as *Henry V*). What is most striking, though, is the implicit apology in it for the unfortunate accident that had caused the withdrawal of the ur-*Henry IV* in 1596, but had also happily resulted in its very successful rewriting followed by the sequel that was now on the stage. Actually, this section is the most unassailable piece of evidence for the fact that Oldcastle was the original name of the character later called Falstaff. That the earlier name and the earlier play had not been forgotten is shown by the prologue to the Admiral's Men's *First part of Sir John Oldcastle* (written by Anthony Munday and others, and performed late in 1599) accusing the Chamberlain's Men of having presented the Protestant martyr Oldcastle as a "pampered glutton" and an "aged Councellor to youthfull sinne."[18] Here is the promise and the apology for the earlier misuse of Oldcastle's name (*2H4,* Epil. 25–30; 1600 Q, sig. L1v):

> our humble Author will continue the storie, with sir Iohn in it, and make you merry with fair Katharine of France, where (for any thing I knowe) Falstaffe shall die of a sweat, vnless already a be killd with your harde opinions: for Olde-castle died Martyre, and this is not the man.

The promise is fulfilled in *Henry V* only in respect to fair Katherine of France, but commentators take comfort from the fact that, though Falstaff is not "in it," at least his death (not in France but in Mistress Quickly's inn)[19] is duly reported, and they proceed to speculate on what is meant by the fatal "sweat": "sweating-sickness" (an epidemic lethal febrile disease that ravaged Europe in the fifteenth and sixeenth centuries), or venereal disease and its treatment by sweating, or, as the first Arden editor R. P. Cowl suggested in 1923, the plague? Very few have heeded Shaaber's shrewd question, after quoting the comments of previous editors "But isn't this the man who 'sweats to death, And lards the lean earth as he walks along'?"[20] The epilogue is merely promising that Falstaff will exhibit further evidence of his cowardice in the French campaign, to the audience's delight. Dover Wilson and Humphreys agree substantially with this reading,[21] but fail to point out a further implication: the disclaimer that follows immediately ("this is not the man") is prompted by the knowledge that the same accusation of cowardice, couched in very similar terms ("sweats to death"), had been leveled at Oldcastle in ur-*Henry IV,* in a passage that survived with a single name change in Part One; it is the passage from the Gad's Hill scene that I had occasion to mention in my first chapter, and which, as Alice-Lyle Scoufos suggested,[22] could have been understood as a piece of "grisly humour" at the expense of the historical Oldcastle, who, as the *Book of Martyrs* vividly illustrates, ended his life hung in chains over a burning pyre.

Those lines deserve a closer scrutiny. Prince Hal watches Falstaff and his confederates run away in confusion, "leauing the bootie behind them," and comments to Poins (*1H4*, 2.2.80–82; Q1, sig.C4v):

> awaie good Ned, Falstaffe sweates to death, and lardes the leane earth as he walkes along, wert not for laughing I should pittie him.

Though printed as prose both in the 1598 Quarto and in the 1623 Folio, these are generally acknowledged as three lines of verse surviving from the version of the play in which Falstaff bore the name of Oldcastle.[23] Replacing the later with the earlier name they would scan perfectly:

> Away, good Ned; Oldcastle sweats to death,
> And lards the lean earth as he walks along:
> Were't not for laughing I should pity him.

There is no doubt that the Prince does not seriously think that the fat knight is going to die: "sweats to death" means simply that, being a great coward, Falstaff/Oldcastle is "in a blue (or deadly) funk."

In fact, the last paragraph of the Epilogue of Part Two reveals an even subtler piece of policy (the leading motif of the Henriad). The disclaimer that the Falstaff "dying of a sweat" is not the Oldcastle who "died martyr" is a reminder that the cowardly knight was a stage fiction, "born," as he says (*2H4*, 1.2.188), "about three of the clock in the afternoon" (the time when performances in public theaters began) not as Sir John Falstaff, but as Sir John Oldcastle, and that the name change was forced upon the players.

The addition to the Epilogue must have been written while *Henry V* was at an advanced stage of "plotting" though only a few parts of it had as yet been fully developed. Several critics, including Dover Wilson, surmise that some of the incidents and speeches meant for Falstaff were transferred to Pistol when it was decided *in extremis* to leave Falstaff out of *Henry V*. Why this belated decision? The most common explanation is that Falstaff's part had been created for the clown Will Kemp; when Kemp left the Chamberlain's Men in 1599 to be replaced by Robert Armin, Shakespeare had to omit his part and introduced instead the role of the Welshman Captain Fluellen, cut to measure for Armin. I have no quarrel with this second explanation, though I am convinced that Falstaff's part was never meant for the clown Kemp, but for another "principal actor," such as John Heminges or John Lowin. Otherwise, why did Shakespeare create such typically Falstaffian roles as those of Sir Toby Belch and of Parolles in later plays, where the new clown Armin's parts are surely those of Feste in *Twelfth Night* and of Lavatch in *All's Well that Ends Well?*

I offer another reason for Falstaff's disappearance, connected with the misapprehension involved in his name that I discuss later.[24] Surely Shakespeare (or his audience) could not keep completely separate the Falstaff of *Henry IV* from the historical Fastolf or Falstaff whose cowardice had caused Talbot to tear the emblem of the Order of the Garter from his knee in *1 Henry VI.* Now, after writing the Epilogue to *2 Henry IV,* Shakespeare, in collecting material for the play on the famous victories of Henry V, learned from the historians that, in spite of his later misbehavior, the supreme Honor of the Garter had been conferred upon that same Fastolf/Falstaff for his gallantry at the battle of Agincourt, which was to be the central event of the new play of *Henry V.* How could Shakespeare keep his promise of showing on the stage Falstaff "dying of a sweat" on this occasion, unless he explained that it was a case of homonimy—in other words that, once again, "this was not the man," neither Oldcastle nor Fastolf? The only way to make it clear was not to have him at all at Agincourt, and simply to report that the "old man" rejected by Henry at the end of the previous play had died.

A further example of Shakespeare's theatrical policy is the solution he found to keep, at least in part, the promise already made to the audience in the Epilogue to *2 Henry IV.* He saw that after all the expression "die of a sweat" could be taken in a literal sense, and had the Hostess announce (*H5,* 2.1.118–19) that Falstaff was "shaked of a burning quotidian tertian"; is not this a form of "sweating-sickness"? And the sweat with the approach of death would turn from burning to cold, "and so upward, and upward, and all was as cold as any stone" (2.3.25–26). From hot to cold: we are reminded of Northumberland's incredulous exclamation on learning of his son's death (*2H4,* 1.1.50): "Of Hotspur, Coldspur?" In fact, thanks to the formidable vitality that Shakespeare had endowed him with, this was not to be the last metamorphosis of the character who had already turned from Oldcastle into Falstaff. Through a devious parallel route, involving an anglicized Italian "bravo" and the cowardly knight who was disgartered in *1 Henry VI*, Sir John Falstaff was to turn up again in Windsor, as the knight of the Garter Inn.

Part 2
The Knight of the Garter Inn

4

Falstaff's Ancestry:
From Verona to Windsor

Many characters in Shakespeare's plays have become human archetypes (to use Jonson's words in the commendatory poem prefixed to the First Folio) "not of an age, but for all time," and indeed, not of a country but for all mankind. Sir John Falstaff is perhaps, if not the best known, at least the most endearing of them. But which is the Falstaff that haunts the collective imagination? The Falstaff triumphantly replacing the unfortunate Old-castle in Part One of *Henry IV* is not exactly the same person, a type of Old Mortality rather than of the clowning morality Vice, pathetically rejected at the end of Part Two. This is by no means all. Another Falstaff had appeared in an earlier Shakespearean history, *1 Henry VI*, as a Garter Knight whose shameful behavior was exposed by the British hero of the Hundred Year War, John Talbot. But, from an early time, audiences were assured that, once again, "this is not the man": in the same way as the Falstaff who was to "die of a sweat" under Henry V must not be identified with the heroic historical Oldcastle, the Falstaff of the time of Henry VI was, in fact, a different person, the cowardly historical Sir John Fastolf recorded in later chronicles. We will discover[1] that this disclaimer—Falstaff has nothing in common with Fastolf—needs at least as much qualification as that Falstaff has nothing to do with Oldcastle, especially if we take into account a fourth Falstaff, who must have put in an appearance in a Garter entertainment presented at Westminster in 1597.

The fat knight that caught the communal imagination, the archetypal Falstaff known the world over, though, is something of a compound figure, based on yet another, a fifth Falstaff, seen not so much against the circumscribed background of English history, but rather in the context of a farcical comedy located in the village of Windsor, the site of his last transformation. The merit for the popularity of this view is not so much Shakespeare's as of the genius of Giuseppe Verdi who, at the end of his life, composed his first comic opera, boldly entitled *Falstaff:* the author of the libretto, the poet and musician Arrigo Boito, in adapting for Verdi *The Merry Wives of Windsor,* managed to incorporate in the figure of the hero the essential features of the Falstaff of *Henry IV.* But I suggest that the debt Falstaff owes to Italy is not only the posthumous one to Verdi's opera: a partly Italian ascendancy can be found for at least three of his original reincarnations.

The Garter Comedy

The Merry Wives of Windsor provides glimpses of the life of a small community, comic intrigues and deceptions, small virtues and vices that could be found in any place in the world; were it not that we are constantly reminded, even by the name of its inn, that Windsor is a very special village—a royal seat, the seat, in fact, as the last act abundantly emphasizes, of the most ancient and exalted chivalric Order in the Realm of England, the Order of the Garter.

That is why the comedy has been called a "Garter play." The definition is deceptive. If it is meant to designate a play that celebrates wholeheartedly the values represented by the Honorable Order of the Garter, then *Merry Wives* does not fit. The only Shakespearean work to which the definition could be applied is the lost (if it ever existed) entertainment presented at Westminster on 23 April 1597 on the occasion of the feast of the Order, which is discussed in my next chapter. But if we take it as referring to the plays showing Shakespeare's attitude toward the chivalric ideals extolled in the time of Elizabeth, then several others should be added to the Windsor comedy: apart from those explicitly mentioning the Garter to brand people unworthy of it *(1 Henry VI, Richard III),* indirect and, in fact, subversive allusions to the Elizabethan chivalric myth are scattered through such different plays as *A Midsummer Night's Dream* and perhaps *Twelfth Night*[2] and *1 Henry IV,* whereas even *Henry V,* presented as a straightforward celebration of the positive values of knighthood, may be read in a very different light, as the triumph of policy.[3]

The Merry Wives of Windsor has been linked with the person of the Queen herself, through the legend according to which Shakespeare wrote the play in a fortnight because Queen Elizabeth wanted to see "Falstaff in love." John Dennis was the first to report, in the preface to his adaptation of *Merry Wives* published in 1702, that "this comedy was written at [Elizabeth's] command, and by her direction, and she was so eager to see it acted, that she commanded it to be finished in fourteen days." This was improved upon, seven years later, by Nicholas Rowe in the introduction of his edition of Shakespeare in 1709, telling how Queen Elizabeth "was so well pleased with that admirable character of Falstaff, in the two parts of *Henry IV*, that she commanded [Shakespeare] to continue it for one play more, and to show him in love." The legend has no historical foundation, but cannot be totally dismissed, because it effectively reflects the general attitude toward the contents of the play. In fact, *Merry Wives* bears all the marks of improvisation, reintroducing, apart from the hero himself, some characters (Mistress Quickly, Justice Shallow, Lieutenant Bardolph, Ancient Pistol and Corporal Nym) already familiar to Elizabethan audiences from their previous exploits in the Histories; but the author seems uncertain about how to integrate them into the plot—they are placed in supporting roles, at times unconnected with the main action, which takes a different turn, bringing to the fore a new set of characters. On the other hand, *Merry Wives*, with its constant mention of local place-names and customs (the most brilliant invention being the Garter Inn, where Falstaff lodges), and with the final celebration of the Queen and of the Order of the Garter, is considered an exception among Shakspeare's comedies—the only one that forsakes the Italian models that, as Leo Salingar convincingly demonstrated,[4] conditioned the writing of the early comedies not only through borrowed plots and situations, but also in dramaturgic technique.

English Comedy and the Italian Connection

Salingar actually singles out *Merry Wives* to illustrate the strength of the Italian influence in the sort of play that seems least amenable to it.[5] On the other hand, Jeanne Addison Roberts, attempting to place the play within the context of Shakespeare's work, finds it

> a play which is not aberrant, trivial, essentially Italianate, nor predominantly farcical. I have no wish to claim that it is a great play, but it is a thoroughly English comedy which fits closely into the texture of the poet's works of 1594–99.[6]

Though insisting on its "Englishness," this view has the merit of not trying—as some have done[7]—to enlist *Merry Wives* among the forerunners of the mainstream of English domestic or City comedy, a genre that was to find its most gifted practitioners in Ben Jonson and Thomas Dekker, Thomas Heywood and Thomas Middleton. In fact, in comparing the work of the latter dramatists with that of Shakespeare, what is most striking is not the similarity, but the substantial difference in the behavior of the characters. Main plot and subplot (the merry wives and the love story of Fenton and Anne Page), once shorn of local references, have little in common with the graphic presentation of the life and interests of the English middle class offered by the authors of City comedies. English local color and the celebration of such national institutions as the Order of the Garter appear in it as hardly more than a decorative superstructure, and their superficial nature is revealed as soon as we try to explore the real origin of the basic situations of the play.

Source hunters have looked for the models on which Shakespeare had based them, but, apart from some marginal details, they have been unable to find any in native English narrative or dramatic tradition. The most obvious source of the main plot of *Merry Wives* is a novella (with no known English translation) from *Il Pecorone* by Ser Giovanni Fiorentino, in the same way as the supporting structure of *The Merchant of Venice* is another story (also untranslated) from the same collection. Characteristically, in Shakespeare's adaptation, the Italian story undergoes a thorough cleansing process: for all the talk of "horns," no adultery is consummated in the play, whereas in the Italian source, the jealous husband is not only repeatedly deceived and betrayed, but also ends up bound as a madman, in such desperate plight that the wife's lover takes pity on him and decides to leave the town for good.

This process of moral cleansing is a recurring feature of English stage adaptations of Italian realistic plots, but far too little notice has been taken of it in dealing with the influence of Italian drama on the theater of Shakespeare's time. Louise Clubb, referring specifically to Salingar's analysis of Italian techniques in *Merry Wives*, notices a central process between the choice of source and the finished play, "comprising contaminatio, patterned complication, and variation of theatergrams." Surely, what I have called the "cleansing process" should go under this last heading. She concludes:

> Unlike most Italian playwrights and most scenario-smiths, Shakespeare never repeats himself; each play, distinct even from those of his other plays nearest it, is like a solution to a problem in theatrical genre. The system that generated such problems and concomitantly offered terms and a process for their solutions was one made in Italy, but enlarged and used wherever in Europe Renaissance drama flourished.[8]

Merry Wives is, perhaps, an imperfect solution to its specific problem of genre, and the reasons for the imperfection will appear from the analysis of its genesis that takes up most of my next chapter. As for the "complication" of the multiple plots, it is, for the same reasons, not as well "patterned" as it should be. On the other hand, there is no doubt about it presenting a remarkable "contaminatio" of genres, which has given rise to the dispute over its Englishness in contrast with the Italianate elements in it, elements that are in the greatest possible evidence in Shakespeare's plays nearest to it in time, belonging one and all to a dramatic genre that characterizes Shakespeare's production of comedies from 1595 to at least 1601, from *The Merchant of Venice* to *Twelfth Night*, and beyond: the so-called romantic comedies. It is a genre close to that of the "romances," the label under which it is now customary to group Shakespeare's last plays, from *Pericles* to *The Tempest*;[9] but the romantic comedies differ from these because they lack the element of wonder, whereas the festive mood prevails (in spite of the ambiguous or bitter notes in such characters as a Jaques or a Malvolio), together with the constant play on disguise and the celebration of young love, so that each of the romantic comedies ends not with a single marriage, but with the union of a number of happy couples.

Fair Verona and Romantic Comedy

There exists, however, an earlier comedy that is considered, by general consent, the forerunner, or rather the first Shakespearean example, of this genre: *The Two Gentlemen of Verona*, written in the early fifteen-nineties. The plot, the themes, the situations of *The Two Gentlemen of Verona* have been traced to a number of sources, both classical and modern, narrative and dramatic, but in all of them the backgrounds, the scenes of the action, are imaginary lands projected into the past. Why did Shakespeare transfer (albeit rather confusedly) the characters to Venetia and Lombardy, Verona and Milan, with Mantua thrown in for good measure, and, in between, a forest that is undoubtedly Sherwood Forest, peopled as it is by gentlemen-outlaws who choose the Veronese nobleman Valentine as their new Robin Hood? Why did he name Verona in the title of the play? The explanation must be looked for on two levels: on the level of unmediated influence there is no doubt that, at the time of devising the new comedy, he had been reading Arthur Brooke's poem *The Tragical History of Romeus and Juliet*, which was to be the single source for his Veronese tragedy, and the places mentioned in that poem must have appeared to him suitable locations for a story of love intrigues, though with a happy instead of a tragic ending. But there is also another type of explanation that requires a different approach.

Shakespeare, from his very first experiment in this genre, conceived of the love comedy—the romantic comedy—as of something typically Italian, and this induced him to choose Italian names for the main characters and, at least in the earliest examples, Italian locations for the action. The reason must be looked for in the origins of romantic comedies on the English stage, and the key to it may be provided by the title itself of *The Two Gentlemen of Verona*, a title that recalls that of another comedy which had enjoyed the privilege of being performed at court before Queen Elizabeth some ten years earlier.

Munday, Shakespeare, and *The Two Italian Gentlemen*

The only extant edition of this comedy is dated 1585, and the full title runs:

> Fedele and Fortunio. The deceites in Loue: excellently discoursed in a very pleasant and fine conceited Comoedie, of two Italian Gentlemen. Translated out of Italian, and set downe according as it hath beene presented before the Queenes moste excellent Maiestie.[10]

Though *The Two Italian Gentlemen* was published anonymously, there is evidence that its author was that exceptional jack-of-all-trades called Anthony Munday—an extremely versatile playwright, who in two very successful plays[11] enriched the Robin Hood legend, by identifying the outlaw who robbed the rich to help the poor with a nobleman forced to retire to the forest by the evil practices of Court and Clergy; he was a novelist in his own right and translator of voluminous French romances, pamphleteer and historian, deviser of pageants for the London City guilds, and government informer against English Roman Catholics. A man who, whereas, on the one hand, he had caused through his accusations the execution of Edmund Campion and other Catholics (and boasted of the fact), on the other, presented the figure of Sir Thomas More in the best play ever written about the Catholic martyr in such a favorable light that Elizabethan censorship prevented its performance.[12] It was apparently on that occasion that Shakespeare's and Munday's paths crossed for the first time, when Shakespeare was called upon to rewrite a scene that might have disturbed the censor;[13] several years later it was Munday who severely castigated Shakespeare and his fellow Chamberlain's Men for their disrespectful presentation on the stage of the protestant martyr Sir John Oldcastle;[14] in the meantime Shakespeare, when writing *The Merchant of Venice,* may well have remembered some incidents in Munday's original novel *Zelauto or the Fountain of Fame,* based on the same novella from *Il Pecorone* that is the main source of the play.

Fedele and Fortunio, or the Two Italian Gentlemen, was written when Munday was hardly twenty-five, possibly as his first attempt at playwriting and intended mainly as a literary exercise. The plot is based on the rivalry between the two young gentlemen Fedele and Fortunio for the love of a gentlewoman, Victoria; the supporting roles are provided by Virginia, a young lady secretly in love with Fedele, Attilia and Pamphila, the maids of Victoria and Virginia, Fedele's tutor Pedante, the braggart Captain Crackstone, and finally the go-between Medusa, an expert in magic arts; exactly as in the Shakespearean comedies, after a whole sequel of errors, disguises and love deceits, the story ends in no less than four happy marriages: Victoria with Fedele, Virginia with Fortunio, Attilia with Captain Crackstone, and Medusa with Pedante.

The play is now remembered, if at all, as one of the rare Elizabethan translations of Italian plays,[15] though Salingar,[16] after quoting Stephen Gosson's well-known statement in his *Plays Confuted* (1582), "bawdy Comedies in Latin, French, Italian and Spanish have been thoroughly ransacked to furnish the Play houses in London," comments: "though only one sure example is known, Anthony Munday's *Two Italian Gentlemen* (c. 1584), from a comedy by Pasqualigo." I suggest that, inadvertently, by devising this play, Munday had founded a new dramatic genre, and that this is the original model of Shakespeare's romantic comedies.

Translated Out of Italian: Commedia Erudita into Romantic Comedy

Young Anthony Munday, when writing his new script, had no other aim than that of providing a fairly sophisticated and partly Italianate English audience with a recent example of Italian comedy: hence, the words "Translated out of Italian" on the title page of the printed text. In 1579, on his way back from Rome, where he had been a student in the Catholic English College[17], Munday stopped briefly in Venice, and there he must have picked up the newly printed second edition of *Il Fedele, Comedia del Clarissimo Luigi Pasquàligo* (the Venetian nobleman Count Alvise Pasqualigo)—a typical "commedia erudita," a dramatic genre practiced by the most eminent Italian men of letters, fusing together classical reminiscences, literary subtleties, and unrestrained bawdiness.

Il Fedele was first published in 1576, then in 1579, and again later in 1589 and 1606, and enjoyed the distinction of a Latin translation by Abraham Fraunce, published in England in 1582 under the title of *Victoria*.[18]

Munday wanted to present the English Court with an English version of the Italian comedy, a version not devoid of literary refinements, but closer to Elizabethan theatrical practices. In fact, Munday's is not so much a translation, as an adaptation with radical changes of Pasqualigo's original. Pasqualigo's play is far from being a romantic comedy on the "deceits in love" happily concluded by the union of four loving couples. Vittoria is no simple maid uncertain in her choice between two suitors: she has a husband significantly called Cornelio ("corna," of course, are "horns"), and freely dispenses her favors alternately to her lovers Fedele and Fortunio, so that, when one of them, jealous of the other, threatens to reveal her behavior to her husband, she makes no scruple of offering herself to the boastful henchman Frangipietra to have the inconvenient lover suppressed. On the other hand, lustful Virginia has a tryst with Fortunio, mistaking him for Fedele in the dark, and only the unexpected arrival of her father forces a marriage between the two. The only other marriage in the Italian play is that between Vittoria's maid Attilia and Fedele's servant Narciso. And in the end Vittoria once more accepts Fedele as her lover, in spite of her earlier attempt to have him killed; her change of heart springs from her gratitude to the man, who manages to hoodwink her husband into believing in her innocence and married chastity. All this is seasoned with the menial loves and intrigues of a number of servants, and with lengthy tirades on the nature of love and on female inconstancy and promiscuity, placed mainly on the lips of the pedant Onofrio. Verbosity, a tendency to use quotations and sententious arguments, are shared by all characters, branding *Il Fedele* as a typical "commedia erudita."

Munday's so-called translation is, in fact, a total metamorphosis. He has shorn the comedy of minor characters and intrigues, preserving only what must have seemed to him the most amusing situations, translated into a different context determined by the suppression of a fundamental theme: adultery. For instance, in Pasqualigo's comedy Fedele, to convince Cornelio of his wife's unfaithfulness shows him his servant Narciso in disguise coming out of Vittoria's house, where he had met her maid Attilia. The disappearance in Munday's version not only of Cornelio but also of Narciso calls for a substantially different solution: in the English version Fedele, to get rid of his rival Fortunio, must make him believe that Victoria is promiscuous and, therefore, shows him Pedante in disguise coming out of Victoria's house (that he had entered as a beggar) and boasting of having enjoyed her. This is a return to the traditional situation of the false meeting of lovers in order to discredit an innocent woman, the most famous example of which is the story of Ariodante and Ginevra in the fifth canto of *Orlando Furioso,* a situation that was to be reproduced in every detail in Shakespeare's *Much Ado about Nothing.*

Munday gave the English audience the impression that the new kind of comedy that he had presented at Court was a faithful reproduction of the Italian model, and it was assumed that the play of the Venetian nobleman Pasqualigo was the model for romantic comedy, whereas, in fact, such comedy was native to England, the more or less casual result of Munday's endeavors at cleansing for an English audience the loose morality of Italian "commedia erudita." It was therefore natural for English playwrights to think of the new "romantic" plays as Italian-style comedies, and not only to locate them in Italy or other southern countries, but also to draw their plots and situations from Italian *novelle* or at least from stories of obvious Italian origin. Hence, such titles as *The Two Gentlemen of Verona* or *The Merchant of Venice* (based on a novella in *Il Pecorone*), and *Much Ado about Nothing* is directly derived from a novella by Bandello of which there was no English translation.

Frangipietra into Captain Crackstone

In spite of the Italian or Italianate background of romantic comedies, a common characteristic of them all is the introduction of markedly English elements in the comic roles. Not only in the case of the typical London night watch appearing in the Messina of *Much Ado,* but also in the other romantic comedies, the clowns, the shrewd or silly servants, have names and use a language that characterizes them as belonging to the small world of Elizabethan

London. In other words, the "lazzi" in the Italian plays, ultimately derived from the "commedia dell'arte," are transferred or rather transmuted into the language of the society in which Shakespeare and his audience moved. Also in this respect it was Munday's *The Two Italian Gentlemen* that provided the model for the "contaminatio" of English humor and Italian comedy. One character that he created deserves particular attention. In reducing the acting roles and reorienting the plot of Pasqualigo's original version, Munday developed only two of the secondary characters in the Italian play at the expense of all the others. The longest role, in his version, is that of Pedante—the counterpart of Onofrio, whose irrepressible verbiage had already been emphasized by Pasqualigo; but the second longest role in Munday's play is that of a character which, in Pasqualigo's, appeared briefly in only two or three scenes: the braggart Frangipietra, sketchily presented by Pasqualigo in terms of "commedia dell'arte" rather than of "commedia erudita." Frangipietra is a "bravo" ready to sell himself to the highest bidder, rough in behavior and language, meant only to expose Vittoria's unscrupulousness in hiring him as an assassin. By translating Frangipietra into Crackstone, Munday created instead a fully rounded character, partly based on contemporary everyday experience: unlike Frangipietra, Crackstone, as he himself tells the audience, is an army sutler who, by "nicking them of their measure [. . .] got so much gain That I bought this apparel of a captain that was slain,"[19] so that he is now accepted by everybody as something of a war hero and, by telling his imaginary war exploits, he moves among the better sort and can confidently accost "proper gentlewomen," even if at times he has to seduce their maids first.

In other words, Pasqualigo's disreputable henchman, the Italian "bravo," through the assumed traditional role of "miles gloriosus," has become the martial model for adventurous young men, and to stress this new position Munday has invented for him a high-sounding language, mixing together military boasts, dog Latin, new polivalent word coinages worthy of Joyce's *Finnegans Wake*, inversions and adaptations of proverbial expressions, and long soliloquies revealing a kind of misdirected self-knowledge. For instance, immediately after having sworn to Victoria that he will kill Fedele, he begins (4.6.1–22):

> Now shall my valerosity appear unto all,
> How I can kill men and serve a woman at her call.

and boasts of having "put cities into sacks and make thousands to yield." But then he thinks it over:

> To bring Fedele to the counter is but to fight with a fly:
> There is neither praise, pride nor providence in the victory.
> Therefore take heed, Crackstone, what you do.
> You hazard your good name; your honour stands on tip-toe.
> To kill a gentleman that never ought me malice is more than
>   cruelty,
> And to kill him for a woman will bring me utterly to infancy.
> Shall I kill him then? Peradventure yea. Shall I let him go?
> Peradventure I may, peradventure no.
> O single device! Here is a brain, I believe,
> Able to shoot birdbolts of inventions from my hand into my sleeve.
> I will make a great noise before Victoria's door in the street,
> As though at this present with Fedele I did meet.
> Then will I run to her house amain
> And make her believe that Fedele is slain.
> Then before that she hear news of his life,
> I'll have her to the priest and make her my wife.

Here are the boasts, the arguments about honor, the devices used when caught red-handed, by that "squire of the night's body" whom his followers call Captain, who, out of Sir John Oldcastle, developed into Sir John Falstaff. Munday, by transforming the common braggart of Pasqualigo's comedy into the eloquent, self-important Crackstone, familiar counselor of adventurous young men, has created the typically English prototype of the boon companion of Prince Hal, which Shakespeare further enriched by making him more mature in years and much ampler in size, as well as by compounding the *maschera* of the Italian "bravo" with the Morality Vice and the Lord of Misrule out of the native English tradition. Sir John Falstaff is the heir of Captain Crackstone, fully transplanted into English soil. Besides, the language that Munday devised for him furnished Shakespeare with some suggestions for the "irregular humorists" surrounding Prince Hal in the two Parts of *Henry IV.* Crackstone not only provided the general outline of the character of Falstaff, but also prompted the creation of Pistol with his emphatic doggerel and his high-sounding misquotations, and Mistress Quickly with her gift for transforming pretentious malapropisms into ever new polisemic inventions.

I have tried to trace the route from the Italian "commedia erudita" of a Venetian man of letters, to English romantic comedy that, because of Munday's manipulation, was thought of in terms of comedy on the Italian model; that is why romantic comedies are generally set in an imaginary Italy, which may at times be called Illyria, or even, when the romantic comedy pattern became a vehicle for a more complex inner dialectical process, Roussilion *(All's Well That Ends Well)* or Vienna *(Measure for Measure)*. From its first appearance the Italian-style romantic comedy enriches its Italianate cast and locale with the addition, mainly in the comic or clownish roles and in the representation of everyday life, of characters, attitudes, and allusions closely connected with the small world of Elizabethan street life (Speed and Launce are the only two non-Italianate names in *Two Gentlemen of Verona*). Details that are so obviously English that Shakespeare, finding in the prototype of romantic comedy—Munday's *Two Italian Gentlemen*— the character of Crackstone (the only Italian name in the play that is translated into English),[20] did not transfer him into one of his romantic Italianate comedies, but promoted him to the role of leading character in two of his *English* Histories, the two parts of *Henry IV.*

The Road to Windsor

In spite of the fact that Salingar had pointed out thematic affinities between *The Two Italian Gentlemen* and *The Two Gentlemen of Verona*,[21] and Daniel Boughner had underlined the kinship between Pasqualigo's Frangipietra and Falstaff, showing how both, when in danger, discourse on the subject of honor,[22] this aspect of Falstaff's ancestry has been obscured even by some of the supporters of the direct or indirect Italian origin of *The Merry Wives of Windsor*. It was assumed at one time that the comedy was a hasty reelaboration, at the Queen's command, of *The Jealous Comedy* performed for Henslowe by the combined Admiral's and Strange's Men on 5 January 1593 (a lost play that may or may not have been written by Shakespeare himself, "based on some Italian tale".)[23] The lost comedy must have been modeled on one of the numerous versions of the story of the Pedant (not of the bragging soldier) in love; it so happens that an authoritative scholar, Oscar James Campbell,[24] hit on the analogy with Munday's *The Two Italian Gentlemen,* but he saw the character of Falstaff not as developing from that of Crackstone, but as a laborious adaptation of that of Pedante, and remarked on the similarity of their soliloquies, though acknowledging that "in this play, however, the pedant is not completely disgraced, largely because Captain Crackstone, the braggart soldier, becomes the principal object of ridicule." Campbell, noticing what he considers relics of pedantic forms in Falstaff's language—the result, in his opinion, of the process of adaptation from the original pedant to the boastful knight—does not seem to realize that such rhetorical flourishes were traditionally shared, though with subtle differences, by the pedant and the "miles gloriosus"—witnesses the two champions of high-falutin' rhetoric in *Love's Labour's Lost,* Holofernes and Armado.

What remains true is that *The Merry Wives of Windsor,* built on the basic scheme of the multiple *beffa,* is an Italian-style comedy in English dress. What singles it out from Shakespeare's romantic comedies is not so much the Windsor locale, as the insistence on the *beffa*—a typically Italian feature—not as subsidiary or incidental, but as the central theme of the plot. As prominent is the invention of diversified languages for the different characters (from the Frenchified English of Doctor Caius to the Welsh accent of Sir Hugh Evans, the pompous rhetoric of the Host of the Garter, the equivocations of Mistress Quickly during the Latin lesson to little William Page): these linguistic mannerisms, though beautifully integrated in the English context, are the direct inheritance of the Italian "commedia erudita," a genre in which Count Alvise Pasqualigo was but a follower in the steps of Pietro Aretino and of Bibbiena, of Ludovico Ariosto and the Sienese Accademici Intronati, not to mention Niccolò Machiavelli.

Shakespeare's road from Verona (in his first romantic comedy as well as in his one lyrical tragedy) to Windsor is, in fact, a tortuous route, with many bypaths and diversions: after calling at Padua, Venice, and Messina, and before paying flying visits to imaginary Arden and Illyria, at least some of the company took a detour to Eastcheap, Shrewsbury, and Gloucestershire, but they were to meet again at their final destination, royal Windsor, where Captain Crackstone, in his third reincarnation as the poor knight Sir John Falstaff, was to witness a peculiar travesty for his own benefit of the rites of the Most Honorable Order of the Garter.

5

Reconstructing the Garter Entertainment at Westminster on St. George's Day 23 April 1597

Most recent editions of *The Merry Wives of Windsor* (with the notable exception of George Hibbard's New Penguin of 1973) accept the date of 23 April 1597 for the first performance of the play, as part of the Garter feast celebrated at Westminster, when George Carey, second Baron Hunsdon, the patron of the company of which Shakespeare was a sharer, was one of the five newly elected knights solemnly invested by Queen Elizabeth with the Order of the Garter. This view was first put forward by Leslie Hotson in his *Shakespeare versus Shallow* (1931), but the most cogent arguments in favor of it were those advanced in 1962 by William Green, in a painstaking study[1] minutely reconstructing on the basis of contemporary historical documents the ceremonies held on that occasion, to show that the performance of a play containing a celebration of the Order of the Garter would have been most appropriate after the supper held at Westminster in honor of the new knights on the evening of 23 April. In fact, though some kind of entertainment would be in order at such a time, no extant document mentions it or specifies its nature; and, at all events, entertainments offered on such occasions were generally in the form of masques rather than two-hour plays. Was, then, the Garter entertainment a much shorter dramatic piece that only some time later was partly incorporated in a full play for the public theatre?

Garter Play and/or Garter Entertainment

The main stumbling block met by the supporters of 1597 as the date of composition of the whole play of *The Merry Wives*—at a time when Shakespeare might have just completed *Henry IV, Part One,* and changed the names of Sir John Oldcastle, Rossill, and Harvey into those of Falstaff, Bardolph, and Peto respectively—is the presence in it, in very marginal roles, of characters who had become popular only after their appearance in Histories performed not before but after 1597: Shallow and Pistol in *2 Henry IV* (1598), Nym in *Henry V* (1599). Besides, the role of Sir Hugh Evans is a typical vehicle for an actor specializing in the comic Welshman, and this fits the bill of Robert Armin, who had joined the company only in 1599, "creating" the character of Fluellen;[2] and the introduction of Doctor Caius can best be explained in terms of exploitation of the comic French linguistic *pastiche* successfully used in *Henry V.* There are other incongruities: for instance, how comes it that Shallow, described as a justice of the peace in Gloucestershire in *Merry Wives* 1.1.5. (but not in the Quarto version of 1602), as well as in *2 Henry IV,* has now a deer park in Windsor? And why is so little trace left in the play of the episode of the "Germans" who steal the Host's horses, which has been rightly taken as an allusion (appropriate to the Garter entertainment) to the Mömpelgard affair?[3] The only reasonable explanation of these anachronisms and inconsistencies is that *Merry Wives* was a new play hurriedly put together around 1600, incorporating parts of an earlier Garter entertainment, dating back to 1597.

The main reason for considering *Wives* a "Garter play" is, of course, the speech of Mistress Quickly impersonating the Fairy Queen at 5.5.58–79—a speech that does not figure in the 1602 Quarto, suggesting that at least on occasion it was not used in public performances, though the rest of the scene was. The speech is a formal celebration of the Order of the Garter, but it does not place the stress on military virtue and valor as attributes of the Garter knights; by quoting the French motto, *Honi soit qui mal y pense,* it emphasises a different aspect of the virtue expected from the members of the Order. George Hibbard[4] remarks that this speech, and the part of the scene in which it is included

is singularly masque-like. The Fairy Queen, the fairies, the Satyr, Hobgoblin—all these are exactly the kind of figures that are to be found in several of the royal 'Entertainments' that have survived. These entertainments are masque-like shows which were put on for the Queen's amusement when she visited the homes of her more important subjects . . . [In 1591], at Elvetham in Hampshire, the fourth day's proceedings began with a speech from the Fairy Queen, after which she and her fairy maids danced about Elizabeth, and then sang a song in praise of her.

Hibbard concludes:

> It therefore seems a reasonable hypothesis that either Hunsdon or the Queen may well have asked Shakespeare and his company to put together such an entertainment for the Garter celebrations of 1597. It would certainly be something that they could do in a fortnight, and it would fit the occasion. Then later, when it was all long over, Shakespeare, with the economy so characteristic of him, salvaged the entertainment, made the necessary changes to fit Falstaff into it, did not bother to insert indications of Welshness into the Satyr's speeches when they were handed over to Evans, and used it for the denouement of his new comedy. It is not a theory capable of outright proof, but it is more consistent with the play . . . than is Dennis's story.[5]

Falstaff and the 1597 Garter Entertainment

My only disagreement with Hibbard's theory concerns the "fitting" of Falstaff into the new play, which implies that the figure of the fat philandering knight was not present in the earlier Garter entertainment. In the following pages I look for new circumstantial evidence in support of the general view expressed by Hibbard (with the proviso just mentioned), and outline the Garter entertainment presented on 23 April 1597 as distinct from the comedy of *The Merry Wives of Windsor*.

The basic issue, I feel, has been obscured by the fact that, whereas a very great deal of attention has been rightly paid to the relationship between the Shakespearean comedy and the other Falstaff plays, to establish, among other things, their chronological sequence, too little account has been taken of the emergence and development of the character of Falstaff and his companions. In the first place, as Hibbard noted, royal entertainments for particular occasions were generally much shorter than regular plays, and all or mostly in verse. *Merry Wives* instead has, by far, the lowest percentage of verse (12 percent, including Pistol's doggerel) of any Shakespeare play. The only partially versified scenes in it—apart from the masquelike Garter celebration and the exposure of Falstaff at 5.5.40–105—are those connected with the Fenton–

Anne Page love story and parental interference (3.4.1–21 and 67–94), the Pages's and Fords's preparations for the Herne the Hunter's masquerade in Windsor Forest at Falstaff's expense (4.4.6–16, 26–79 and 82–90; Evans's prose interventions in the scene look like later interpolations), Fenton's arrangements with the Host of the Garter for the elopement with Anne Page during the fairies masque (4.6.1–55), and Fenton's and Anne's reappearance after the masque, celebrating their happy union against the miseries of enforced marriage, as part of the final rejoicing and merry making (5.5.216–45).

Hibbard's suggestion that *Merry Wives* was hastily written (either at the Queen's command or just as a money-making proposition) in 1599–1600 accounts for the presence of these verse passages: together with the "Garter speech," I take them to be the only parts of the play borrowed and adapted (with changes and insertions of new lines) from the entertainment presented by the Hunsdon Men before the Queen at Westminster Palace on 23 April 1597 for the Feast of the Garter—an appropriate occasion for the company in that one of the five new Knights of the Garter elected that day was their patron, George Carey Lord Hunsdon.

A most suitable central feature of an entertainment devised for such an occasion would be a masque in which the Fairy Queen (an obvious allegorical projection of Queen Elizabeth) ordered her court to make the necessary preparations for the installation ceremony that was to take place a month later in Windsor Castle (see 5.5.56–74). And it was for such a queen to stress, among the duties of the Garter knights, the virtue of chastity.[6] The latter would suggest the subject matter for the antimasque[7] that was to complete the day's entertainment. This view is supported by the verse sections from the Garter show incorporated in *Merry Wives*. The Fenton-Anne story underlines the dangers to married chastity represented by parentally enforced marriage (see 5.5. 218–27), whereas Falstaff is the knight unworthy of the Order of the Garter because he is "corrupt, and tainted in desire." The general outlines of the Garter entertainment of 1597, then, were based on the honorable deception of the parents practiced by a pair of lovers and the punishment of a corrupt knight unworthy of the Order, culminating in the celebration of the Garter virtues and of the "radiant Queen" who "hates sluts and sluttery" (5.5.46). There was no room in this simple scheme for the "irregular humourists" of the Henry plays: in the original Westminster masque (corresponding to *Merry Wives,* 5.5.37–102), the speakers were the Fairy Queen and her followers, awkwardly replaced in the later comedy version by Mistress Quickly, Evans, and Pistol utterly deprived of their individual speech mannerisms, whereas Falstaff's prose speech at ll.81–82, detecting the Welsh accent of a "fairy," is an obvious later interpolation, intruding in a perfect rhymed couplet spoken by the original fairies.[8] But before attempting an ampler reconstruction of the 1597 entertainment, let us take a closer look at its hero, or rather anti-hero. The question to be asked at this point is: Which Falstaff in Windsor?

There is reason to suspect that not only the unworthy knight, contrary to Hibbard's conclusions, figured already in the 1597 entertainment, but also that his name was from the beginning Sir John Falstaff. The very idea of presenting a knight unworthy of the Order would have suggested that name. The only other occasion in the whole of Shakespeare's work when the Order of the Garter and the duties of its members are mentioned at some length is in *1 Henry VI,* 4.1.9–47, the scene in which the English national hero Talbot tears the Garter from Sir John "Falstaffe"'s leg for "Prophaning this most Honourable Order."[9]

Fastolf and Falstaff versus Oldcastle— and a Grant of Arms

A difficulty arises at this point. In Shakespeare's *1 Henry VI,* the name of the historical character who deserted the battle of Patay "without any stroke stricken," as Hall and Holinshed put it, though he had been "the same year for his valiantness elected to the order of the garter," is consistently spelled "Falstaffe"; but in the chronicles from which Shakespeare drew his information it is given as "Fastolf," "Fastolfe," or "Fastollfe." He was actually "disgartered" not by Talbot but by Bedford, the Regent of France, and Shakespeare, though taking a hint from it, decided to ignore the further report by the chroniclers that "Sir John Fastolffe" was able to justify his behavior at Patay, and "was restored to the Order against the mind of the Lord Talbot." A fact not unknown to the librarian Richard James when, in his epistle to Sir Henry Bourchier,[10] he tried to disentangle both the Oldcastle/

Falstaff muddle and the question of how Falstaff could be alive under Henry VI if he had died under Henry V:

> In Shakespeare's first shewe of Harrie ye fift, ye person with which he vndertook to playe a buffone was not Falstaffe, but Sr Ihon Oldcastle, and . . . offence beinge worthily taken by personages descended from his [title . . .], the poet was putt to make an ignorant shifte of abusing Sr Ihon Fastolphe, a man not inferior [of] Vertue though not so famous in pietie as the other.[11]

The learned librarian simply imputes to Shakespeare's ignorance the confusion of the names and of the characters. Editors of the plays defend him from the accusation by maintaining that he had actually made a clear distinction between the two, later obliterated by a scribe or a compositor of the First Folio. True it is that, though *1 Henry VI* was already very successful on the stage in 1592, it appeared in print only posthumously in the 1623 Folio, so that the latest editor of the play, Michael Hattaway, is justified in stating:

> Throughout the Folio text and in all editions of the play before that of Theobald he is called 'Falstaffe', because, no doubt, of scribal or compositorial confusion with the famous character in *1* and *2 Henry IV*.[12]

Perhaps "no doubt" is supererogatory. The question of the name has been amply debated,[13] and I find far from improbable the suggestion that the altered spelling may be authorial. Because in any case Sir John was meant to be the type of the knight unworthy of the Garter, Shakespeare may well have seen from the beginning, when he first introduced him as such in *1 Henry VI*, the allusive possibility offered by a slight variant in the name, from Fastolf to Fall-staff or False-staff, branding him as a false bearer of the emblem of military valor, staff or shaft being synonymous of spear—a notion familiar to the playwright whose grandfather Richard's family name is set down in the Snitterfield court rolls as both Shakeschafte and Shakstaff.[14] The significance of Shakespeare's own surname in connection with the name of Falstaff has been remarked upon by T. W. Herbert and Harry Levin,[15] who detect a suggestion of cowardice both in "Shake-spear" and in "Fall-staff," to which Roberts,[16] in the second instance, adds that of impotence, appropriate to the final scene of *Merry Wives*. This is perhaps going too far. Shakespeare was certainly aware of the martial quality of his family name, the very opposite of "Fall-" or "False-staff," and at all events its full significance was brought home to him by the grant to his father John and to "his children yssue and posterite" of

> This shield or cote of Arms, viz. Gould, on a Bend Sables, a Speare of the first steeled argent. And for his creast or cognizaunce a falcon his winges displayed Argent standing on a wrethe of his coullers: supporting a Speare Gould steeled as aforesaid sett vppon a helmett with mantelles & tasselles.[17]

The grant by the Garter principal king of Arms is dated 20 October 1596, and it must have amused Shakespeare to include, in an entertainment for a Garter celebration that he was called to devise shortly afterward, the type of the unworthy knight: the derogatory implications of the name borrowed from that of the dishonorable historical character who had put in a brief appearance in *1 Henry VI*, suggested for him a coat of arms with a falling spear— in ironical contrast with Shakespeare's own.

It is likely, therefore, that the royal entertainment on 23 April 1597 presented a knight actually called Falstaff, as yet a different person from what we know as the Sir John Falstaff triumphantly appearing in the two parts of *Henry IV* in 1597–98. But we should recall once again that, when a play on Henry IV was written and possibly performed in 1596, the "villainous abominable misleader of youth" was not called Falstaff but sir John Oldcastle, and that the use of his name was objected to by the powerful Brooke family, connected with that Oldcastle whom John Foxe had celebrated as a protomartyr of the Protestant religion. William Brooke Lord Cobham, Lord Chamberlain from August 1596 till his death in March 1597, was in a particularly strong position to exact the suppression of a play containing a slanderous presentation of his ancestor. I have already illustrated[18] my view that the replacement of the "Oldcastle" version of *Henry IV* (originally, I believe, a single play) was a fairly laborious task undertaken in late 1596 or early 1597. The Garter entertainment presenting the Sir John Falstaff revived from *1 Henry VI* was produced at a time when Shakespeare was busy rewriting with considerable changes and amplifications the role of Oldcastle in the new version of *Henry IV*, and looking for a new name for the knight. Why not adopt the name used on the occasion of the Garter Feast, which added to Sir John Falstaff's earlier taint of cowardice the further imputation of lechery and corruption?

In other words:

1. The Sir John Falstaff exposed at Windsor in the Garter entertainment of 23 April 1597 was the same as the one even more dishonorably exposed in some brief scenes of *1 Henry VI.*
2. The Garter entertainment gave Shakespeare the idea of replacing with "Falstaff" the name of "Oldcastle" that had given offense to his descendants, in the rewriting of *Henry IV* as a new play or plays in 1597–98.
3. When, for whatever reason, Shakespeare was asked in 1599–1600 to write a comedy about the *new* Falstaff who had been successful in the two parts of *Henry IV,* he remembered the earlier Garter entertainment located in Windsor and, fusing together old and new, transferred to Windsor—improbable as it may appear—the irregular humourists that in the Histories had haunted Eastcheap, Gadshill, Gloucestershire, and even the fields of France.

A Chronology of Shakespeare's Work on the Histories

Here is a detailed prospect of the chronological sequence of the plays and entertainments in which Shakespeare had a hand between 1596 and the end of the century, apart from the romantic comedies and *Julius Caesar:*

1596
Early in the year Shakespeare writes for the Chamberlain's Men a remake of the first part of *The Famous Victories of Henry V,* under the title of *Henry IV,* covering events from the first rebellion in the North to the king's death, stressing the wildness of Prince Hal and his reformation, and developing the characters of his companions, Rossill (Sir John Russell), Harvey, Pointz, and particularly Sir John Oldcastle. The play is successfully staged.

23 July: The Lord Chamberlain, Henry Carey, first Baron

Hunsdon, dies. The company passes under the patronage of his son, George Carey, second Baron Hunsdon, and is renamed the Lord Hunsdon's Men.

August: William Brooke, seventh Baron Cobham, is appointed Lord Chamberlain. He objects to the presentation on the public stage of Sir John Oldcastle. The play is withdrawn. Shakespeare undertakes to rewrite it for the next season, developing the role of Oldcastle under a less offensive name.

At about this time Queen Elizabeth decides to fill the next year the vacancies in the Order of the Garter by electing new knights, among whom George Carey, Lord Hunsdon. The latter commissions from his company an entertainment in view of the festivities for the investiture, on Saint George's day 23 April 1597.

1597

5/6 March: William Brooke Lord Cobham dies.

17 April: George Carey Lord Hunsdon is appointed Lord Chamberlain.

23 April: In a solemn ceremony at Westminster Queen Elizabeth invests five new Knights of the Garter: Frederick Duke of Württemberg (formerly Count Mömpelgard) in absentia, Thomas Lord Howard de Walden, George Carey Lord Hunsdon, Charles Blount Lord Mountjoy, Sir Henry Lee. Though there is no record of it, it is likely that, after the supper that followed evensong, the Chamberlain's Men presented an entertainment celebrating the Order and Queen Elizabeth in the person of the Fairy Queen, while the comic antimasque would center on the figure of a knight unworthy of the Order because of his sexual uncleanness (a homage to the cult of chastity promoted by the virgin queen). The knight was named after the infamous Sir John Fastolf (False-staff) disgraced for his cowardice in *1 Henry VI*.

At the same time, Shakespeare was busy rewriting the play on Henry IV and looking for new names to replace those used the year before. He gave the main character the name and title that had been revived on the occasion of the Garter entertainment: Sir John Falstaff. The new play—published the next year simply as *The History of King Henry IV*—was presented successfully on the stage.

1598

In view of this success, the Chamberlain's Men commissioned and presented a sequel to it (see chapter "Reconstructing the Ur-*Henry IV*" above), ending with the promise of a third Falstaff play, *Henry V*, where "Falstaff shall die of a sweat," and with an apology for calling him Oldcastle in an earlier version.

1599

When it was presented at the newly built Globe, the rewriting of the second part of *Famous Victories* as *Henry V* did not keep the promise of showing Falstaff, possibly because Shakespeare had become aware of the historical Fastolf's gallant behavior at Agincourt, but introduced new comic roles: Fluellen the Welshman, suited to Robert Armin, the new Clown of the company; corporal Nym, with his recurring tag "That's the humour of it";[19] and the French Dauphin.

1599–1600

Presumably for commercial reasons, rather than obeying a Royal command, Shakespeare devised a new comedy centering on the figure of Falstaff, partly incorporating the Garter entertainment of 1597, exploiting some typical situations in Italian and English novels, and reintroducing the most successful comic figures in the recent Histories: Bardolph (1H4), Pistol (2H4), Nym (H5), Shallow (2H4), a new Mistress Quickly that shared only her linguistic oddities with her previous namesake, the well-meaning Welshman (Fluellen = Evans), the pompous Frenchman (Dauphin = Caius).

The Brook/Broome Affair and the Poor Knight of Windsor

The result of the process I have summarized was *The Merry Wives of Windsor*, a dual-purpose comedy, for both court presentation (even if we do not credit the story of the royal command) and the public stage. The Garter masque (albeit the Fairy Queen of the original Garter entertainment was redimensioned as Mistress Quickly, the Satyr as Evans, and Hobgoblin as Pistol) would please both audiences, whereas the "Latin lesson" (4.1) is obviously meant only for the sophisticated court audience rather than for the more general one of the Globe—and on occasion also the Garter speech by the Queen of Fairies might have sounded out of place. This accounts for the two major omissions (the whole of 4.1 and the speech at 5.5.58–76) in the 1602 Quarto of the play, which appears to be a "reconstructed" text based on a public performance. The Folio text reflects instead the full version of the 1599–1600 play, including the substitution of Ford's assumed name "Broome" for the original "Brooke" to avoid any further possible offence to the Cobham family.

The Brooke-Broome change has caused serious difficulties to the supporters of 1597 as the date of composition of the entire comedy, including editors of the play like H. J. Oliver[20] and the most recent, T. W. Craik,[21] as well as Jeanne Addison Roberts.[22] If we acknowledge instead that Shakespeare wrote the play, as distinct from the Garter entertainment, in 1599–1600, the use of the assumed name Brooke for the suspicious Ford can be seen as the author's little revenge for having been forced by the earlier Lord Cobham, William Brooke, to substitute the name of Oldcastle, whereas the further change to Broome may well have been caused by the resentment of the surviving Brookes. But the change itself from Brooke to Broome could be a further insult to the Brookes: Ernst Honigmann[23] has shown that in 1595 the wife of a Mr. Broome was, with her husband's consent, under the "protection" of William Brooke. Honigmann comments: "having been ordered to remove the name Brooke from *Merry Wives*, Shakespeare or his colleagues added insult to injury by dragging in the Broomes. This would have been a clever counterthrust; the Cobham-Mr Broome-Mrs Broome triangle is repeated in the play, with Cobham (i.e. Oldcastle, i.e. Falstaff) offering to cuckold 'Mr Broome.'"

It is now time to leave the Falstaff of *The Merry Wives*—a pale reflection of the one appearing in the two Parts of *Henry IV*—and to go back to the other Falstaff, modeled in the 1597 entertainment not on the Sir John Oldcastle who had been Prince Hal's companion in *The Famous Victories of Henry V*, but on the cowardly Garter knight who had deserted Talbot at Patay in *1 Henry VI*. The lost entertainment can only be reconstructed in its general outlines from hints offered by the later comedy. The first valuable clue is represented by the presence in a secondary role of a new character, the Host of the Garter, and by the choice of the Garter

Inn as Falstaff's permanent lodging in Windsor. The satirical intention is obvious. The poor knights of Windsor were a well-known institution: they were commoners who had acquired their title through services rendered as soldiers, but, having no hereditary property, were kept as Crown Pensioners. Falstaff is one of them—not a nobleman but a retired captain. His lodging at the Garter Inn is a sign of both his frustrated ambition of ranking with the top nobility of the Kingdom (the twenty-six Knights of the Order of the Garter), and his gift for equivocation: being a knight and living at the Garter Inn he could be referred to as "the knight of the Garter."

The Garter Entertainment of 1597—a Reconstruction

From the evidence of the versified parts of the comedy, which were the most likely to have been borrowed and adapted from the earlier Garter Entertainment of 1597, it appears that the latter required a much smaller cast, apart from the fairies in the masque. Granting that the Garter entertainment was built round three main interwoven strands, here are the basic requirements of each of them:

1. Love plot. A young gentleman (=Fenton); a young girl (=Anne Page); the parents of the girl, either one or both of whom wanted her to marry a person of their own choice; the person or persons chosen for her by her parent(s). It is difficult to determine if each of the parents favored a different pretender for the girl (as in *Merry Wives*) or if only one did so. At all events, the love plot did not need more than six actors.
2. The unworthy knight plot. Only two actors were essential: the knight himself, a poor pensioner of Windsor who aspired to a higher rank and saw himself as an irresistible lady-killer; the Host of the Garter Inn, where the knight lodged. The knight wanted to restore his fortunes by seducing the girl's mother and/or other wives of well-to-do Windsor commoners.
3. The "German Duke" plot, intended as a satire on the behavior of the Duke of Württemberg, formerly Count Mömpelg-

ard (see *Wiv.*, 4.3 and 4.5). In fact, there was hardly any need to present on the stage the three other lodgers in the Garter Inn who, under pretense of attending on a German Duke, cheated the Host of his horses; the episode could as well be reported by the Host's servant or tavern drawer. This would explain why, when some years later Shakespeare wrote his comedy, dragging into it Falstaff's companions, Bardolph is very soon transferred from the knight's service to that of the Host of the Garter (1.3.4–19; Folio, sig. D3):

> *Fal.* Truely mine *Host;* I must turne away some of my followers. . . .
> *Ho[st]*. Discard, (bully *Hercules*) casheere; let them wag; trot, trot. . . . I will entertaine *Bardolfe:* he shall draw; he shall tap; said I well (bully *Hector*?)
> . . .
> *Fal. Bardolfe,* follow him: a *Tapster* is a good trade: an old Cloake, makes a new Ierkin: a wither'd Seruingman, a fresh Tapster: goe, adew.
> *Ba[rdolph]*. It is a life that I haue desir'd: I will thriue.[24]

Bardolph had to replace the presumably anonymous drawer bringing the news of the confidence trick played on the Host.

The entertainment may well have begun by introducing the overbearing knight in conversation with the Host of the Garter Inn, laying his plans for the seduction of rich Windsor wives. Mention might have been made on this occasion of his fellow lodgers, the "three Gentlemen" (Quarto version), or "Germans" (Folio) waiting for the arrival of a Duke, along the lines of the short exchange between the Host and Bardolph at 4.3 (Folio, sig.E4):

> *Bar.* Sir, the Germane desires [Germans desire] to haue three of your horses:[25] The Duke himselfe will be to morrow at Court, and they are going to meet him.
> *Host.* What Duke should that be comes so secretly? I heare not of him in the Court: let me speake with the Gentlemen, they speake English?
> *Bar.* I sir? Ile call him to you.[26]
> *Host.* They shall haue my horses, but Ile make them pay: Ile sauce

them, they haue had my houses[27] a week at commaund: I haue turn'd
away my other guests, they must come off, Ile sawce them, come.

Exeunt

Such a short scene, sandwiched between two much longer ones,
the second of which (4.4) begins with exactly the same characters
on the stage who were present at the end of the earlier one (4.2),
looks like an intrusion inherited and adapted from a version in
which the dialogue was part of a different longer scene.

The rest of the Garter entertainment must have interwoven this
slender satirical (and topical) strand with the story of the unworthy lodger in the inn attempting to seduce the mother of the
heroine of what can be considered the main plot line: the love
story of a young girl whose father has different plans for her
marriage. The versified parts of 3.4, reproducing the original love
scene between Anne and Fenton, suggest that Mistress Page is
not so averse to let her daughter have her way: it is Master Page
who has other plans for her. Again, the verse sections of 4.4 and
4.6 indicate the further development of this plot: on the one
hand, the father plans the punishment of the knight who has
designs on his wife (though in the later comedy there is a duplication of the situation, through the introduction of the "Italianate"
story of the deception of the jealous husband); on the other hand,
the young lover enrolls the help of the Host of the Garter to
deceive the father of the heroine. Adding to this the deception of
the Host himself by the followers of the "German Duke," we have
the simple comedy of errors that constitutes the antimasque of
the Garter entertainment. It should be noted that it dispenses
with the Ford/Brooke play of disguises, the hiding of Falstaff and
the other episodes that Shakespeare devised later, when he engaged in the writing of a full-fledged comedy, having recourse to
new Italian sources and to some of the characters that had become
popular by appearing in the Histories he had written in the
meantime.

The Garter masque proper, led by the Fairy Queen, with the
celebration of the Order, the punishment of the unworthy knight
and the triumph of true love against enforced marriage, was the
conclusion of the courtly entertainment offered to the Queen and

to the old and new Knights of the Order on Saint George's day 23 April 1597.

Postscript: The Dual Chronology of the Falstaff Plays

An imperfect consensus. In spite of the assurance by Jeanne Addison Roberts[28] that "we are approaching a consensus on the date" of composition of *Merry Wives*, i.e., 1596–97, even the supporters of a close connection between the comedy as it stands now and the Garter celebrations of 1597, though dismissing as irrelevant the fact that the play was not mentioned by Francis Meres in his *Palladis Tamia* (1598), find it difficult to place it within the sequence of the other Falstaff plays. They are forced to push back to 1596, against all known evidence, the date of completion and stage presentation of both Parts of *Henry IV.* An ingenious compromise is suggested by the editors of the Oxford *Complete Works.*[29] Though accepting Roberts's surmise[30] that to write the new Garter comedy, "Shakespeare interrupted his work on *2 Henry IV* at 4.3" when he "had already invented Shallow and Pistol," they doubt that by April 1597 he could have reached this point in the writing of the history, so they advance the opinion that

> Queen Elizabeth's request for a play on Falstaff in love could have been made in anticipation of a later court performance that Whitehall season (on 26 February 1598). . . . *Merry Wives* could . . . have recollected, rather than anticipated, the Garter ceremonies of spring 1597; the play would still have been written with a court performance in mind, honouring by allusion the company's patron, and satirizing by contrast Henry Brooke, the new Lord Cobham, who would have been instrumental in the censorship of *1 Henry IV.* Shakespeare's composition of *2 Henry IV* would have been interrupted by the request for *Merry Wives*, and *2 Henry IV* as a consequence would not have been completed until spring or early summer of 1598.[31]

The forest of conditionals and subjunctives is a clear indication of strain in devising a solution that, on the one hand, connects the play with a court occasion, and on the other, suggests acceptable dates for the two Parts of *Henry IV.* But why recall a Garter celebration and announce an installation ceremony some ten months after the event? And why borrow from the as yet incomplete and unperformed *2 Henry IV* the characters of Shallow and

Pistol, which the audience would not recognize because they had never appeared before on the stage? Why devise for the occasion of a court play to be performed on 26 February 1598 the new character of Corporal Nym, so obviously intended to satirize the theatrical fashion set by Jonson's comedy of humors—he uses the word *humor* twenty times in eleven of the twelve speeches allotted him—when the earliest possible date of performance of *Every Man in His Humour* is July of that year? Roberts[32] argues that "Shakespeare invented Nym specifically to fill a plot need in *The Merry Wives*," namely, "to balance Pistol"; but that is true of *Henry V* rather than *Merry Wives*.

The Humor of It. In his turn, William Green[33] notices that Nym's well-known tag line or "verbal tic," "that's the humor of it," appearing six times in the Folio text of *Henry V* (and eight in the bad quarto), is instead constantly varied in *Merry Wives*, but in the 1602 bad Quarto of the comedy turns up five times in the form "and there's the humor of it." This is explained by the fact that the reporter of the bad Quarto text of *Merry Wives* replaced the imperfectly remembered varied mentions of humors with a constant formula modeled with a slight variant on the one consistently used in the history play. But it is no proof that the comedy had been written two years before the history; it is more likely that Shakespeare, writing *Merry Wives* shortly after *Henry V*, would deliberately play variations on the tag line already familiar to the audience from Nym's previous appearance in the history play. Corporal Nym, Bardolph, Pistol, and even Mistress Quickly, are no longer full-blown human characters; they are, one and all, in contrast with their appearances in the histories, presented merely as "humours," counting exclusively on their linguistic peculiarities. In fact, *Merry Wives* is Shakespeare's ironical tribute paid to the new theatrical genre of the comedy of humors, and the title page of the 1602 bad Quarto is fully justified in describing it as "Entermixed with sundrie variable and pleasing humours." Shakespeare could neither adopt nor satirize the genre before 1599, when, thanks to Jonson's comedies, it triumphed on the London stage.

Recurring Characters. Green supports his theory on the sequence of composition of the plays (*1 Henry IV*, late 1596; *2 Henry IV*, January–April 1597, completed if not performed; *Merry Wives*, April 1597; *Henry V*, Summer 1599), by producing a "Chart of

Military Titles in the Falstaff Plays," including the characters of Falstaff, Bardolph, Peto, Gadshill, Pistol, Nym.[34] Such a chart, which has to acknowledge the disappearance of any military title in the comedy, except in the case of Nym, is further evidence of the wrongness of the sequence suggested. The omission of indications of rank means simply that they were presented no longer as functionally linked to the action of the play, but as stage figures already well known to the audience from their previous appearances, whereas Nym retained his title because he was a recent addition to the group of "irregular humourists," not yet as familiar as the others. Let us now complete the chart with the designations of the other characters without military rank who figure in more than one Falstaff play, leaving out Gadshill (not a military but merely a "setter," the robbers' decoy, appearing in only one play) and including instead Mistress Quickly, Poins, Doll, Falstaff's page, and Shallow, and place them in what I consider the correct sequence.

Designations of Recurring Characters in the Falstaff Plays

	1H4	*2H4*	*H5*	*Wiv*
FALSTAFF	knight	knight captain	(mentioned)	knight
QUICKLY	hostess married	hostess widow	hostess remarried	housekeeper spinster
BARDOLPH	no mention of rank	corporal	corporal lieutenant	no mention of rank
POINS	gentleman	gentleman	(absent)	(mentioned)
PETO	lieutenant	no mention of rank	(absent)	(absent)
PISTOL	(absent)	ancient lieutenant	ancient lieutenant	no mention of rank
SHALLOW	(absent)	justice	(absent)	justice
DOLL	(absent)	?gentlewoman	(mentioned)	(absent)
FALST'S PAGE	(absent)	boy, page	boy	Robin, boy page
NYM	(absent)	(absent)	corporal	corporal

Quickly Metamorphosed. The transformation of Mistress Quickly is the most striking. If we accept any of the theories maintaining that the whole play of *Merry Wives* was completed by 23 April 1597 (or, according to the Oxford editors, by 26 February 1598) we must accept as well that:

1. Shakespeare created, in the first place, the conventional type of the Hostess, a "most sweet wench" and "an honest man's wife," who has not much to say for herself in *1 Henry IV* (1596–97).
2. When writing the unplanned sequence to that play in 1597–98, he transmuted her into a superannuated widow, a bawd whose delusions of respectability are reflected in her magnificent use of linguistic equivocation.
3. *At the same time,* in *Merry Wives,* she figures as the spinsterish housekeeper of a French doctor in Windsor, using the same language for her side-trade of go-between.
4. Finally in *Henry V,* once again as a hostess, as well as Pistol's wife, "her genius for unintended and unperceived obscenity," in Gary Taylor's words,[35] "helps make her report of Falstaff's death perhaps the most moving . . . messenger speech in the canon."

But if *Merry Wives* postdates *Henry V* the transition from full-blown character to mere stage type or humor, in her case as in that of the other characters borrowed from the histories, is justified.

The Two Chronologies. The attempts at dating the comedy have confused two distinct sorts of chronology: on the one hand, the actual chronology of composition of the Falstaff plays, and on the other, the fictional chronology of the events represented in those plays. For reasons discussed in a previous chapter, Shakespeare had decided not to keep the promise of showing Falstaff in the French campaign, as the Epilogue of *2 Henry IV* had stated. Mindful of the ten-mile banishment from Westminster of Falstaff and his crew at the end of that play, Shakespeare was careful, in *Henry V,* not to specify the location of the inn where Mistress Quickly, now married to ancient Pistol, is plying her trade as a hostess, from whence Falstaff is gathered "to Arthur's bosom," and his followers are summoned to join the French expedition. The mention of Staines at 2.3.2 suggests a place up the Thames to the west of London, at the opposite end from Eastcheap, down the river in the heart of the City. To fit into the play a character meant to mock the growing fashion for "humours" on the stage, Shakespeare created Corporal Nym as the unsuccessful rival of Pistol for the hand of the hostess. Later, though, Nym becomes associated with Bardolph rather than Pistol, because "Nim and Bardolph are sworn Brothers in filching" (3.2.44), which leads to their death, in contrast with Pistol who, as the Boy comments (4.4.69–74), is not a thief simply for lack of courage:

> The empty vessel makes the greatest sound, Bardolfe and Nym had tenne times more valour, then this roaring diuell i'th olde play . . . and they are both hang'd, and so would this be, if hee durst steale any thing aduenturously.

The Boy himself was soon to come to a sad end, cruelly massacred by the French.

Reviving Falstaff. It was Falstaff's absence from *Henry V* that caused the demand—by public theater audiences rather than by the Queen—for a comedy where he would appear again, to dispel the gloomy impression left not only by the announcement of his death, but also by the fate of his followers, including Corporal Nym, a posthumous addition to them. In improvising, at short notice, the new play, Shakespeare was faced with the same sort of problem that confronted many authors of serials and sequels for the press, the stage, or the large or small screen in the following centuries. To justify the revival of his hero, he could not present, as did Conan Doyle at the end of last century, the death of Falstaff, like that of Sherlock Holmes, as mere pretense, nor could he pretend, as did, in more recent times, the harassed scriptwriters of *Dallas,* that Henry the Fifth's famous victories in France, like the death of Bobby Ewing, had never taken place, being merely a hallucination. History left Shakespeare no other choice except that of presenting the comedy, hastily put together from Italianate sources and the recollection of the 1597 royal entertainment where a different Sir John Falstaff had appeared, as a marginal episode in the life of the fat knight, at the time of his banishment from London. The clue was given by Henry's rejection speech (*2 Henry IV,* 5.5.66–70; 1600 Quarto, sig. K4v):

> For competence of life, I will allow you,
> That lacke of meanes enforce you not to euills,

> And as we heare you do reforme your selues,
> We will according to your strengths and qualities,
> Giue you aduauncement.

What other "competence of life" could be offered a discredited and impecunious knight except a pension and a place among the poor knights of Windsor? His companions (the king is addressing Bardolph, Pistol, and the page, as well as Falstaff) would of course follow him there. To them Shakespeare added his latest creation, Corporal Nym (also to keep up the joke about humors); not Poins: already in *2 Henry IV* he is Prince Hal's rather than Falstaff's companion, he is not present at the rejection and does not figure at all in *Henry V.* In *Merry Wives* we are slyly reminded of his different role and status in the passing mention (3.2.73) of the fact that the young gentleman Fenton (not the commoners Pistol and Bardolph) "kept companie with the wilde Prince and *Pointz.*"

Reviving Mistress Quickly. The revival of Mistress Quickly presented a different problem. She had been a hostess in Eastcheap, and in *Henry V* we had seen her in the same capacity, remarried to Pistol, in an unspecified locality necessarily outside London. It could not be Windsor, because the inn there was emblematically called the Garter Inn, and the personality of its Host had already been firmly established in the Garter entertainment of 1597. Shakespeare had no choice but to imagine that, in the interval between the rejection of Falstaff and the preparations for the French campaign, Mistress Quickly had temporarily changed her trade in order to figure plausibly in Windsor. Hence her role as housekeeper and general busybody, a merry former and future wife. Astutely, Shakespeare drops a hint about her future when Pistol, following her off-stage, exclaims (2.2.137–39):

> This Puncke is one of *Cupids* Carriers,
> Clap on more sailes, pursue: vp with your fights:
> Giue fire: she is my prize, or Ocean whelme them all.

The hint is hardly developed in the rest of the play, though Pistol as Hobgoblin partners Quickly as Queen of Fairies in the Folio version of the Windsor forest revels.

In the chronology of "history" Shakespeare has endeavored to insert *The Merry Wives of Windsor* between the action of the Second Part of *Henry IV* and that of *Henry V.* But he could not have done so if, in the chronology of composition, he had actually written the comedy before the last of his "histories" of the Lancastrian cycle.

6

Five Falstaffs and the Countess of Salisbury: *Edward III* as a Garter Play

Alter et idem, always different and always the same: What is the common denominator of the five characters to which, at some stage or other, Shakespeare gave the name of Sir John Falstaff—Fastolf, the cowardly Garter knight in *1 Henry VI;* the former Oldcastle, boon companion of Prince Hal in ur-*Henry IV;* the unworthy knight in the 1597 Garter entertainment; the fat, aging Sir John in the two Parts of *Henry IV;* the poor knight of Windsor's Garter Inn in *The Merry Wives?* Three of them, and especially the first and the last, are associated, albeit in indirect ways, with the great English institution of the Garter, whereas the principle of which it was an emblem, Honor, is the subject of many direct and indirect references in connection with Falstaff's other appearances. Perhaps the reply to the question depends on a closer look at Shakespeare's approach to the institution itself.

A Galaxy of Garters

The Order of the Garter is explicitly mentioned in the whole of Shakespeare's work only three times: in *Richard III,* Richard himself is accused of having dishonored the Order,[1] whereas on the other two occasions it is associated with the typical anti-hero, Sir John Falstaff, though we know that the Falstaff appearing in *1 Henry VI* is actually Sir John Fastolf, a Garter knight expelled from the Order because of his cowardice, and, therefore, at least at first sight, only indirectly and casually related to the one in *The Merry Wives of Windsor,* a play containing a masquelike celebration of the Order just when the fat knight (apparently a "poor knight of Windsor" i.e., a military pensioner) is being exposed to public ridicule.

Garters appear in other dubious contexts.[2] In *The Taming of the Shrew* Petruchio turns up for his marriage disreputably attired "with a linen stock on one leg and a kersey boot-hose on the other, gartered with a red and blue list" (3.2.65–7)—the "list" of the Garter was plain blue, with no red in it. At the beginning of *Henry V* the tying of a garter (though apparently not that of the Order) is ironically associated with "the cause of policy": Canterbury, enumerating the exceptional gifts of the reformed prince Hal, now king Henry V, says (1.1. 45–47):

> Turn him to any cause of policy,
> The Gordian knot of it he will unloose,
> Familiar as his garter.

And may not the mock "cross-gartering" of Malvolio in *Twelfth Night* be an oblique ironical reference to the insignia of the Order? There are two knights in the play, not belonging to the Order: Sir Andrew Aguecheek is a fool and Sir Toby Belch a replica of Falstaff for domestic use; but the apocryphal letter purporting to come from the hand of the Lady Olivia is understood by the steward Malvolio as the promise of new greatness: "I will be proud, I will read politic authors, I will baffle Sir Toby" (*TN*, 2.5.161–2). Falstaff, on learning from Pistol of the death of the old king (*2H4*, 5.3.120ff), had exclaimed: "I am Fortune's steward!" and began offering new honors to all around him.

It is rather surprising that most Shakespearean allusions to the Garter (whether capitalized or not) should be associated with mockery or profanation. This is true also of the very first mention of it, when Talbot, asking for the degradation of the historical Falstaff (or Fastolfe) in *1 Henry VI*, speaks of the virtues of the Order in the past tense (4.1.33–44; 1623 Folio, sig. l3v):

> When first this Order was ordain'd my Lords,
> Knights of the Garter were of Noble birth;
> Valiant, and Vertuous, full of haughtie Courage,
> Such as were growne to credit by the warres:
> Not fearing Death, nor shrinking for Distresse,
> But alwayes resolute in most extreames.
> He then, that is not furnish'd in this sort,

Doth but vsurp the Sacred name of Knight,
Prophaning this most Honourable Order,
And should (if I were worthy to be Iudge)
Be quite degraded, like a Hedge-borne Swaine,
That doth presume to boast of Gentle blood.

Commenting on this episode, Peter Erickson, in a subtle analysis of the implications of *The Merry Wives of Windsor* as a Garter play,[3] remarks that its value as a negative example is shortly after counteracted by the invocation of St. George, the patron of the Order, in the battle cry "God and Saint George, Talbot and England's right" (*1H6*, 4.2.55), which underlines the military and nationalistic meanings of the institution. And, by following up this line, he suggests that also another Shakespearean History should be considered a "Garter play":

The motif is reiterated in *Henry V* in the king's call "God for Harry, England and Saint George!" (III.i.34). The repeated invocations of his great-grandfather Edward III and of the English victory at Crécy, which inspire in Henry V a conviction of entitlement to France, give the play a Garter dimension since the order of the Garter originates with Edward III, who founded it precisely in this military context: "Participation at Crécy is the most immediately striking common factor among the first knights of the Garter."[4]

The Founding of the Order

The recollection of the founding of the Order in a military context is most appropriate to Talbot's speech in *Henry VI* as well as to the battle cry in *Henry V*, but it should be noted that the stress is placed on a quite different aspect of it in the speech of the Fairy Queen in the masque in *The Merry Wives of Windsor*—a survival, as I suggested, of the entertainment offered for the Garter Feast of 1597—ordering the preparations at Windsor Castle for the installation ceremony of the new knights. There is no mention of martial virtues (5.5.65–72; 1623 Folio, sig. F6):

And Nightly-meadow-Fairies, looke you sing
Like to the *Garters*-Compasse, in a ring.
Th'expressure that it beares: Greene let it be,
More fertile-fresh then all the Field to see:

> And *Honi Soit Qui Mal-y-Pence*, write
> In Emrold tuffes, Flowres purple, blew, and white,
> Like Saphire-pearle, and rich embroiderie,
> Buckled below faire Knight-hoods bending knee;

The quotation of the motto of the Garter is a reminder of the legend about the creation of the Order and of the reason for its adoption, a reason unconnected with those conceptions of nobility, valor and courage extolled in the history plays. The legend was first reported by Polydore Vergil, but was best known in Shakespeare's time from the pages of Holinshed's *Chronicles*, which are the main source of his Histories.

Already in the first edition of 1577 Holinshed reports that the Order of the Garter was "devised" by Edward III at the conclusion of a series of "martiall feasts, and iousts, tornaments, and diuerse other the like warlike pastimes," held at Windsor Castle "betwixt Candlemasse and Lent" at the beginning of the eighteenth year of his reign (1344). The account of what is described in the marginal heading as "The occasion / that mooued / K. Edward / to institute / the order of / the garter" (that is reproduced verbatim in the posthumous 1587 edition, except for a few spelling and punctuation variants) is paraphrased with some omissions from a passage in Polydore Vergil.[5] This is Holinshed's reading:

> The cause and first originall of instituting this order is vncerteine. But there goeth a tale amongst the people, that it rose by this means. It chanced that K. Edward finding either the garter of the quéene, or of some* ladie with whom he was in loue, being fallen from hir leg, stooped downe and tooke it vp, whereat diuerse of his nobles found matter to iest, and to talke their fansies merilie, touching the kings affection towards the woman, vnto whome he said, that if he liued, it should come to passe, that most high honor should be giuen vnto them for the garters sake: and there vpon shortlie after, he deuised and ordeined this order of the garter, with such a posie, wherby he signified, that his nobles iudged otherwise of him than the truth was. Though some may thinke, that so noble an order had but a meane beginning, if this tale be true, yet manie honorable degrees of estates haue had their beginnings of more base and meane things, than of loue, which being orderlie vsed, is most noble and commendable, sith nobility it selfe is couered vnder loue, as the poet *Ouid* aptlie saith,
>
> *Nobilitas sub amore iacet.*
> William de Montacute earle of Salisburie king of Man, and marshall of England, was so brused at the iusts holden here at Windsore (as

before ye haue heard) that he departed this life, the more was the pitie, within eight daies after.

Edward III and the Countess of Salisbury

Holinshed had not only omitted some of Polydore's classical references in the passage, but also made an unobtrusive addition to his faithfully reported text: next to the words "some ladie with whom he was in loue" there is the marginal note "The countes of Salisburie"; and attention is drawn to it in the 1587 edition (used by Shakespeare for his Histories) by the introduction of an asterisk in the text. There is no mention of a Countess of Salisbury in Polydore Vergil—but that lady has instead a leading role in the first two acts of the anonymous chronicle history of *Edward III,* a play written and performed in the early 'nineties of the sixteenth century, and in which, by general consensus, Shakespeare must have had a hand. In fact, in recent years there has been a growing tendency to attribute to him a much greater part in the writing of the play than the few scenes traditionally acknowledged as his.[6]

The main argument against Shakespeare's authorship of the play is the fact that it was not included in any of the Folios, nor was it ever mentioned after its second edition in 1599 (the first was published in 1596), until in 1656 the booksellers Richard Rogers and William Ley attributed it to Shakespeare in a highly unreliable list of plays appended to their edition of Thomas Goff's *Careless Shepherdess*—so unreliable that it mentioned as Shakespeare's Marlowe's *Edward II* and Heywood's *Edward IV.* The total disappearance of any mention of *Edward III* after 1599 can be justified on other grounds: on 15 April 1598 George Nicolson sent Lord Burghley a strongly worded letter protesting against the abuse of the Scottish nation on the English stage:

> It is regretted that the comedians of London should scorn the king and the people of this land in their play; and it is wished that the matter should be speedily amended lest the king and the country be stirred to anger.[7]

It is more than likely that the "play" in question was *Edward III,* where the second scene offers a bitterly satirical presentation of King David of Scotland and Sir William Douglas, who are also the object of the pointed irony of the Countess of Salisbury (ll.170–249), while in the last scene of the play King David is led prisoner on the stage (2316–2495).[8] The play was presumably forbidden, and the 1599 reprint can be taken as an attempt by the publisher to get some profit from a play that was no longer to be seen on the stage.[9] The suppression of the play would of course be maintained even more rigidly after the advent, in 1603, to the throne of England, of King James of Scotland, who had originated the initial veto five years before. So after a time the vetoed play would have been completely forgotten, and Heminges and Condell would not include it in the 1623 Folio, as they did those other early histories and comedies that were still alive on the stage.

The Rites of Chivalry

All the same, in view of the time when it was first presented, it is rather strange that a play on Edward III, purporting to celebrate his great achievements and those of his son, the Black Prince, should make no mention of such a central event of his reign as the foundation of the Order of the Garter. From the beginning of her reign, Queen Elizabeth had revived, in the splendid Accession Day Tilts, those rites of chivalry that Edward III had founded, making of them an essential part of the Elizabethan myth of Astraea.[10] As time went on, and the cult of the Virgin Queen was seen with some misgivings, because the lack of direct descendants could well have thrown the country at her death once again into the throes of civil war, all the emphasis was placed—in the fifteen-nineties—on the Order of the Garter, in view of its institutional aims, as set down in the revised statutes of Henry VI:

> To aduance to honor and glory good, godly, valiant, well couraged, wise and noble men for their notable desertes, and to nourishe a certaine amytie, fellowship, and agrement in all honest thinges among all men, but specially among equalles in degre, for they do iudge honor, as surely it is, the rewarde of vertue, and concorde the foundation and enlarger of common weales.[11]

The Garter was a reward not so much of military prowess, as of a virtuous public and private life in the service of the state. The best evidence of this is George Peele's poem, *The Honour of the*

Garter, published in 1593 on the occasion of the installation of the Earl of Northumberland as a Knight of the Garter.[12] In more than four hundred lines of blank verse, Peele recounts in dream form the story of the Order and its foundation; following closely Holinshed's and Polydore's report, he mentions that King Edward III, "disposed to reuell, after he had shaken Fraunce,"

> Found on the ground by Fortune as he went
> A Ladies Garter,

but hastens to say "The Queenes I troe Lost in a daunce," with no mention of the alternative offered by the previous historians: *reginae seu amicae* according to Polydore, *of the quéene, or of some ladie with whom he was in loue*, in Holinshed's more explicit words. Peele was a court poet, ready to second and even forestall his sovereign's wishes.[13] It is perhaps significant that in the very same year 1593 he should have contributed to the poetical collection *The Phoenix Nest* a poem under the title "The Praise of Chastity."[14] Presumably not long after this Shakespeare himself sang the praise of royal chastity in Oberon's words about the "fair vestal thronèd by the West" (*A Midsummer Night's Dream*, 2.1. 155–64):

> But I might see young Cupid's fiery shaft
> Quenched in the chaste beams of the watery moon,
> And the imperial votaress passed on
> In maiden meditation, fancy-free.

Lines written perhaps to atone for presenting in the play the Queen of Fairies (not the Fairy Queen!) in love with an ass.

Peele's celebration of the Garter came no more than a couple of years after Talbot's Garter speech on the stage in a play that, according to Nashe's *Pierce Pennilesse*,[15] had attracted to the theatre "ten thousand spectators at least (at seuerall times)"; and the wording of some parts of it closely anticipates the Fairy Queen's speech in the 1597 Garter entertainment later incorporated in *The Merry Wives of Windsor*. Besides, 1593 or thereabout seems a likely date for the production of the Shakespearean *Edward III*.[16] But the question remains: how can a play on the founder of the

Order avoid, at such a time, any mention, if not of the Order itself, at least of its aims that the Queen was endeavoring to revive?

Edward III, Froissart, and Le Bel

It is well known that the most indubitable Shakespearean scenes of the play are those connected with the episode of Edward's infatuation with the Countess of Salisbury. The episode, in fact, is not to be found in Holinshed, which was the most recent, practically inescapable, source of all history plays. The story of "Howe the kyng of Englande was in amours with the Countesse of Salisbury," instead, is chapter lxxxvii of the *Cronycle* of Jean Froissart in the English translation done at the command of king Henry VIII by John Bourchier Lord Berners (1523–25). That Shakespeare knew the work of the pro–English French historian who had lived at the court of Edward III in the thirteen-sixties is apparent from the words he attributed to the Duke of Alençon in *1 Henry VI* (1.2. 29–31):

> Froissart, a countryman of ours, records
> England all Olivers and Rolands bred
> During the time Edward the Third did reign.

Little notice has been taken of the fact that the allusion is to a rather obscure passage in the second tome of Lord Berners's translation (third and fourth books, published 1525), dealing with events that took place well after "the time Edward the Third did reign," in 1387. Froissart relates a discussion between the king of Navarre and the French on how to resist the invasion of the kingdom of Castile by the forces of John of Gaunt and the Portuguese, remembering that the Spaniards twenty years earlier, in 1367, had been defeated on the same ground by the Black Prince at the battle of Najera. To counteract the misgivings of the French allies, a Spaniard, the earl of Lune, maintains that the English are no longer what they used to be:

> the prynce at the batayle of Marres [Najera, 1367] had x.M [ten thousand] speres and vi.M [six thousand] archers; they were suche men that there were a iii.M [three thousand] of them every man worth a

Rowlande or an Olyvere. But the duke of Lancastre hathe none suche.[17]

Only a very attentive reader of both tomes of Froissart, and one specifically interested in the reign of Edward III and in the legendary exploits of his son the Black Prince, could have noticed this belated reference to them. Most appropriately, Shakespeare, like Froissart, placed this high praise of the valor of the English on the lips of a foreign nobleman.

The heroic events of the time of Edward are found instead in the first tome (first and second books) of Froissart/Berners. The episode of the Countess of Salisbury is meant as an open confutation of the lurid account given by the hostile Jean Le Bel in his *Vrayes Chroniques* (ca1355–60) of "Comment le roy Edowart forfist grandement quant il efforcha le contesse de Salbry";[18] according to Le Bel, it was in honor of the Countess, whom he loved, that Edward had arranged great festivities in London in August 1342,[19] and only two years later, while the earl of Salisbury was on a mission in France, he visited her in her castle, and raped her:

l'enforcha à telle doulour et à tel martire qu'onques femme ne fut ainsy villainement traittiée; et la laissa comme gisant toute pasmée, sanant par nez et par bouche et aultre part. . . . Puis s'en parti l'endemain sans dire mot.[20]

A passage that sounds like a crude anticipation of the narrative of the rape in Shakespeare's *Lucrece*, when, after the event, Tarquin (ll.736–42)

> like a thievish dog creeps sadly thence,
> She like a wearied lamb lies panting there;
> He scowls and hates himself for his offense,
> She desperate with her nails her flesh doth tear;
> He faintly flies, sweating with guilty fear,
>   She stays, exclaimimg on the direful night.
>   He runs, and chides his vanished loath'd delight.

Froissart's narrative is a far cry from this. Actually, commenting in a later chapter on the English king in a version of his chronicles that is preserved only in manuscript, Froissart is very critical of Le Bel:

Vous avés bien chy dessus oy parler coumment li roys englès fu ena-
mourés de la comtesse de Sallebrin. Toutesfoix, lez cronikez monsei-
gneur Jehan le Bel parollent de ceste amour plus avant et mains
conveignablement que je ne doie faire; . . . je vous di, se Dieux m'ait,
que j'ai moult repairiet et converssé en Engleterre en l'ostel du roy
principaument, et des grans seigneurs de celui pays, més oncques je
n'en oy parler en nul villain cas; . . . Ossi je ne poroie croire, et il ne
fait mies à croire, que ungs si haux et vaillans homs que li roys d'Engleterre est et a esté, se dagnaist ensonniier de deshonnerer une
sienne noble damme ne un sien chevalier qui si loyaument l'a servi.[21]

According to Froissart, Edward fell in love with the Countess during a visit to her castle in the North that had been besieged by
the Scots; but when she rejected his advances, "the kyng departed
all abasshed."[22] Only some time later,

for the loue of this lady, and for the great desyre that the king had
to se her, he caused a great feest to be cryed, and a justyng to be
holden in the cyti of London in the myddes of August [1342?].[23]

But the king's aim was defeated:

All ladyes and damoselles were fresshely besene accordyng to their
degrees, except Alys countesse of Salisbury, for she went as simply as
she myght, to the intent that the kyng shulde nat sette his regarde on
her, for she was fully determyned to do no manner of thynge that
shulde tourne to her dyshonour nor to her husbandes.[24]

After this the Countess disappears altogether from Froissart's
Cronycle, and neither historian associates her name or the feasts
at which she was present with the establishment of the Order of
the Garter, which in a later chapter Froissart briefly reports as
occurring during a solemn feast proclaimed for the occasion on
St. George's day (23 April) 1344, when Edward willed "the quene
to be ther aco[m]panyed with .iii.C. [three hundred] ladyes and
damosels all of noble lynage and aparelled acordingly."[25]

Bandello and Painter

Froissart's version of the story in the French original seemed
so good an example of the triumph of honor and chastity to the
Italian storyteller Matteo Bandello, that he included it as the

twenty-fifth in the second part of his *Novelle* (1554), and five years later Boaistuau gave it the place of honor as the very first of his *Histoires Tragiques extraites des oeuvres italiens de Bandel;* in turn, William Painter faithfully translated it from the French, as the forty-sixth novel in the first volume of that precious mine of subject matter for the Elizabethan dramatists, *The Palace of Pleasure* (1566):

> A King of England loued the daughter of one of his noble men, which was Countesse of Salesbury, who after great sute to atchieue that he could not winne, for the entire loue he bare her, and her greate constancie, hee made her his queene and wife.[26]

The title itself of Painter's novel suggests the extent of the unwarranted amplifications and arbitrary deformations that Bandello had introduced into Froissart's report. The most striking is the new happy ending, by which, ignoring the existence of Queen Philip, who gave Edward no less than seven male children (some of whom were to determine the fate of England for the next two centuries), the king married the Countess shortly after the death of her husband in France. Painter himself, fairly well versed in the history of England, was aware of the liberties taken with it by Bandello, and put in a disclaimer in the introduction to his novel, by listing some contradictions with historical facts, among which

> that the said Edwarde when hee saw that hee could not by loue and other perswasions attaine the Countesse but by force, married the same Countesse, which is altogether vntrue, for that Polydore and other aucthors do remember but one wife that hee had, which was the sayde vertuous Queene Philip, with other like defaults: yet the grace of the histoire for all those errours is not diminished.[27]

Painter's interest lay in the moral implications of this reversal of the story of Lucrece, ending with the reformation of the English would-be Tarquin. As for the fate of the poor Earl of Salisbury, it is hardly mentioned (Holinshed, though listing him among the original twenty-six first Knights of the Garter, had curiously reported his death following "bruises" received during the tournaments that had preceded the incident of the garter and the foundation of the Order): what is stressed is the relationship of the Countess to her father, the Earl of Warwick. In the Bandello/Painter version, after the death of the Earl of Salisbury on his way back from imprisonment in France, the Countess moved to her father's house in London. Whereupon the king,

> seing all thing (as he thought) to succede after his desire, . . . ordeyned many triumphes at the Tilt and Torney, Maskes, Momeries, Feastes, Banquettes, and other like pastimes, whereat ladies accostumablye doe assemble.

But when the lady still refused to become his mistress, the king turned to her father, who was a member of his Privy Council, asking him to induce his daughter to yield to his will. Bandello/Painter devote many pages to the description of the anguish of the Earl of Warwick, torn between his duty and devotion to his king and the prospect of being "a shameless Pandarus of my daughter's honor." It is the Countess herself who solves all doubts by threatening to kill herself rather than lose her honor. At this point the king,

> consideringe the inuincible constancie and chastitie of the Countesse, vanquished by remorse of conscience, ioyned with like pitie, taking her by the hand, said: "Rise vp Lady, and liue from henceforth assured: for I will ne yet pretende all the dayes of my life, to commit any thing in you against your will."

and calling upon all Peers of the Realm, Edward asks the Archbishop of York to join him and the Countess in marriage. The tale ends with the description of the imaginary sumptuous nuptials, "on the first day of July then folowinge," of the happy couple, and of the coronation of the new Queen.

The Earl of Warwick and the Ethics of Power

There is no doubt that the authors of *The Raigne of King Edward the third* knew and used the story. The rest of the play takes from Froissart several episodes and incidents that are not in Holinshed (though in one or two cases the reverse is true),[28] but for the Countess episode Froissart's narrative is amplified with extensive borrowings from Painter's story, albeit the authors, mindful of Painter's own warning about the historical inaccuracies in it, endeavor to respect both the moral aims pursued by the teller, and the historical "truth" of Froissart's report. They eschew the most patent "errours," that is, the marriage of king and Countess and the death abroad of the Earl of Salisbury (who actually appears later in the play in another "exemplary" episode taken from Froissart, where it involves a completely different character),[29] and they compress the action, so that there is no move from the castle in the north to London, but everything takes place in the two days while the king is a guest of the Countess. They do instead take from the story the figure of the king's secretary, whom they develop into a courtier to whom Edward commissions the writing of a love sonnet to the Countess, a delightful satire on a current literary fashion; and they borrow from it the decisive circumstance for the king's reformation, that is, the Countess's threat to kill herself. But the crucial loan from the story is the interview of the king and Warwick, the Countess's father, and then the meeting of father and daughter. In the story Warwick is torn between his revulsion from playing pandar to his own child, and the king's argument that by so doing

> you shall winne the heart of a king, to be vsed as you liste for euer. And the more the thing shall seeme harde, difficult or painefull, the greater shall your merite be, and the more firmely shall he be bounde, whiche doth receiue it. Consider then my Lorde, howe profitable it is, to haue a king at your commaundement.[30]

The play alters slightly the terms of Warwick's predicament, by introducing a more strictly political element: only after having extracted from him a renewed oath of absolute allegiance, the king intimates:

> therefore Warwike if thou art thy selfe,
> The Lord and master of thy word and othe,
> Go to thy daughter and in my behalfe,
> Comaund her, woo her, win her ani waies,
> To be my mistres and my secret loue.
>
> (ll. 675–79 [2.1])

Warwick's problem has become one of divided allegiance—to the king, on the one hand, and to his own and his daughter's honor, on the other—in the same way as in the collaborative play of *Sir Thomas More*, likewise written around the year 1593, the allegiance to the king was contrasted with that to More's own conscience.

More specifically, the debate is on the ethics of power, its use and misuse and abuse. It is precisely the subject of Shakespeare's (only) political Sonnet 94:

> They that haue powre to hurt, and will doe none,
> That doe not do the thing, they most do showe,
> Who mouing others, are themselues as stone,
> Vnmooued, could, and to temptation slow:
> They rightly do inherrit heauens graces,
> And husband natures ritches from expence,
> They are the Lords and owners of their faces,
> Others, but stewards of their excellence:
> The sommers flowre is to the sommer sweet,
> Though to it selfe, it onely liue and die,
> But if that flowre with base infection meete,
> The basest weed out-braues his dignity:
> For sweetest things turne sowrest by their deedes,
> Lillies that fester, smell far worse then weeds.

On another occasion I have argued that the echoes of this scene of *Edward III* in the sonnet go well beyond the fact that its last line is identical with the conclusion of Warwick's lengthy speech (defined earlier as "a spacious field of reasons") on the misuse of power, pronounced when the Countess rejects the king's message that he, in duty bound, had delivered to her.[31] The sonnet concentrates into fourteen lines an argument developed in more than one hundred in the play.

Chivalry: the Education of Princes

Warwick's speech, and the following scene between the king and the Countess, are the first and most open statement of what Tillyard recognized as the unifying structural element of the play:[32] the education of princes. In fact, the theme is pursued throughout. The authors went to the trouble of borrowing a marginal episode found only in Froissart (Book I, chapter cxxxv: "Howe sir Gaultier of Manny rode through all Fraunce by save conduct to Calys"), changing the names of the characters involved to provide another example of the education of a Prince, this time Charles, the French Dauphine: Villiers, a French nobleman, teaches a lesson to Prince Charles by threatening to go back to

prison unless the Prince grants the Earl of Salisbury a safeconduct, which Villiers had promised to procure in exchange for his
freedom—see *Edward III,* 4.1 (1625 – 68) and 4.3 (1754–809), as
well as 4.5 (2056–103) where the Prince teaches the same lesson
to his father the King of France, who wants to detain Salisbury
on his way to join King Edward at Calais.

But the most significant episode of all in the same line—an
episode not found in any of the sources—is that of the ceremonial
arming of the young Black Prince before the battle of Crécy (3.3,
1442–98), and, two scenes later (1572–625), of his solemn knighting, after triumphing against tremendous odds in a battle during
which his father had firmly refused to send him reinforcements,
because

> if himselfe, himselfe redeeme from thence,
> He will haue vanquisht cheerefull death and feare,
> And euer after dread their force no more.
>
> (1561–63)

These central martial and ceremonial scenes are clearly celebrations of the principles and of the forms presiding over the institution of the Order of the Garter. In this sense *Edward III* is as
much a Garter play as *Henry V,* with which it has frequently been
associated, notably by Muriel Bradbrook, who pointed out the
striking structural similarities between the two plays.[33] In fact,
from an ideological point of view, *Edward III* prefigures the structure not only of *Henry V,* but also of the whole Henriad. The
reformation of King Edward, controlling his sensual involvement
in the first two acts of the play, anticipates Prince Hal's transformation, in *1 Henry IV,* from the dissipated companion of Falstaff
into the heroic fighter at Shrewsbury. The "education" of the
Black Prince in the third act of *Edward III,* through his father's
lesson on the requirements of the true knight, corresponds to the
king's deathbed admonitions to Prince Hal in *2 Henry IV.* The
parallel between the celebration of Edward's hard won military
triumphs in France in the last two acts of the early play, and those
of the king in *Henry V,* is obvious; and both plays close on acts of
magnanimity by their respective English kings: Edward by par-
doning the burghers of Calais and reuniting with his Queen,
Henry by atoning for the ruin caused to France, so eloquently

described by Burgundy (*H5*, 5.2.23–67), through his marriage with fair Princess Katherine.

Edward III as a Garter Play

Because of the virtues it unambiguously celebrates, *Edward III* is more of a Garter play than *Henry V,* in spite of the fact that the Order is never mentioned in it, not even in the presentation of the "moral" episode of the Countess of Salisbury, a name that Holinshed (though ignoring the story itself) had associated with the circumstances of the founding of the Order. I suggest that the original intention of the dramatists who undertook to present a play on the glorious reign of King Edward III was to include the central symbolic event of the institution of the Order of the Garter, which summed up the ideals and the principles on which the greatness and the concord of England was based. When they searched Holinshed's chronicles for an account of the event itself, they found the marginal hint to the Countess of Salisbury, whose garter picked up by the king from the dance floor had suggested the name and the motto of the first and most honorable chivalric Order of Britain. But though William Montacute (Montague) Earl of Salisbury, the husband of the Countess, was listed among the original founding members of the Order, there was no further mention of the Countess herself in Holinshed. With a view to finding out the role played by the Countess, they turned to the other best-known chronicle of the time, Lord Berners's translation of Froissart. It reported the story of Edward being "in amours" with the lady, as an episode totally unconnected with the founding, three years later, of the Order of the Garter—an event that was treated briefly, in half a folio column, with no explanation of the reason for the choice of the name for the Order.

This curious game of mutual reticence by the two major historical witnesses—each of them omitted some essential circumstance stated by the other—must have induced the dramatists to celebrate the significance of the Garter not directly but by implication, by extracting from Froissart's account of Edward's involvement with the Countess (though unrelated to the legend of the institution of the Order), and even more from the ampler and richer version in the Bandello/Painter story, those elements (especially in Warwick's and in the Countess's speeches and behavior) that underlined the principles of honor on which the Order, never openly mentioned, was founded. Besides, by culling out of Froissart and emphasizing those episodes (the Salisbury safeconduct, the burghers of Calais) that extolled the Garter virtues, and by adding others out of their own imagination (the knighting of the Black Prince), Shakespeare and his collaborators created in *The Reign of King Edward the Third* the first structurally integrated Garter play. Unfortunately, its satirical treatment of the Scots prevented the survival of the play as the necessary prelude to the second cycle of Shakespeare's histories, devoted to the immediate descendants of King Edward, from Richard II to Henry V. That cycle was completed in 1599, shortly after the suppression of *Edward III* that should have marked its triumphant beginning. *Henry V* may well appear to celebrate precisely the principles listed in the reformed statutes as the aims of the Order of the Garter, and the same is true of the last three acts of *Edward III*.

It is reasonable to consider all this group of plays dealing with English history, from the French conquests of Edward III and the Black Prince at Crécy and Poitiers, to the famous victories of Henry V at Harfleur and Agincourt, as Shakespeare's "Garter cycle." But at the one end of this impressive cycle, the episode of the Countess of Salisbury shows how honor could be manipulated by power, whereas at the other end, the duplicity of King Henry's language,[34] signally in the night scene (4.1) with privates Bates, Court, and Williams, reveals another form of manipulation. And in between lies the "original sin" of the deposition of Richard II, followed by the complex theatrical and censorial vicissitudes that accompanied the dramatic presentation of the unquiet reign of Henry IV. The result was the emergence of Sir John Falstaff as the anti-heroic hero of the five-part dramatic saga on the Honor of the Garter. Right at the center of it is placed, as the ultimate evidence of Shakespeare's dramaturgic policy, Falstaff's catechism on honor. And the last touch of policy is the addition of a "coda" (like the "jig" that concluded all shows, whether tragic or comic, in Elizabethan public playhouses) to the historical cycle, in the form of the *Most Pleasant and Excellent Conceited Comedy of Sir John Falstaff and the Merry Wives of Windsor* (such is the title of the 1602

Quarto), the only play in which the French motto itself of the Order of the Garter is deliberately mentioned.

Honi Soit Qui Mal y Pense: Sexuality and Power

The ambiguity of the motto has been frequently commented on: it defines by contraries the principles on which the chivalric Order is based—not "Honour to him that acts nobly," but (in Holinshed's translation of the motto) "Shame come to him that euill thinketh." The Knights wore a **lady's** garter, an emblem of sexual rather than military conquest, and the justification offered by Polydore Vergil and Holinshed by way of the Ovidian quotation, *Nobilitas sub amore iacet,* Nobility is subject to love, is rather lame, because the love in question is not, in the specific instance, "being orderlie used," but rather subject to the prevarications of power. The double association of the Garter with Honor on the one hand and with Lust on the other, suggested to Shakespeare an equally ambivalent attitude to it. In one respect, his allusions to the emblem of the Order are in line with those of the courtiers who, seeing King Edward pick up a lady's garter from the dance floor in Windsor, "found matter to iest, and to talke their fansies merily."[35] The most direct references are jocular or rather ironical, associating the emblem with negative examples: Richard III and the two Falstaffs—the cowardly knight of *1 Henry VI,* and the poor knight of Windsor in *The Merry Wives.* Surely, the list of the garter worn by the latter would not be plain blue—the color of the Honor of the Garter—but blue and red—the color of Lust— like the one worn by Petruchio at his wedding (*Shr.* 3.2.66–67), all set to tame the shrew who was going to become his wife.

This leads to the other, much more serious, aspect of Shakespeare's attitude to the Garter myth. It is strictly linked with a theme present in Shakespeare's work from the beginning—the relationship of sexuality and power, whether political or patriarchal—both in tragedy (Tamora and Aron in *Titus Andronicus*) and in comedy (Petruchio and Katherina in *The Taming of the Shrew*), and most evident in the first cycle of histories, through the creation of the character of Queen Margaret in the three Parts of *Henry VI*, and in Richard's power of seduction in *Richard III*.

Roman Lucrece

The mutual impact of sexuality and power is explored, above all, in Shakespeare's nondramatic poetry, in the triangular relationship poet/noble patron/mistress, and more pointedly in the two classical myths—parallel by contrast—that he chose as subjects of his two longer poems, sexuality as power in *Venus and Adonis*, power over sexuality in *Lucrece*. Whether or not we agree with Ted Hughes[36] in considering Venus the Goddess whose sexual power, in the form of a boar, slays Adonis to revive him as a flower, the myth that is most thoroughly dissected and is present throughout Shakespeare's dramatic works is that of Lucrece. In its crudest form it had inspired the story of Lavinia in *Titus Andronicus*, as the counterpart to that dark Venus, Tamora; and it was mentioned in a playful mood in *The Taming of the Shrew*, when Petruchio states his determination to marry Katherina against her will (2.1.292–96):

> If she be curst, it is for pollicie,
> For shee's not froward, but modest as the Doue,
> Shee is not hot, but temperate as the morne,
> For patience shee will proue a second *Grissell*,
> And Romane *Lucrece* for her chastitie.

In the same jocular vein, we should remember that the Lady Olivia in *Twelfth Night* had chosen the picture of Lucrece as the emblem on her seal. It is exactly the sight of "the impressure her *Lucrece*, with which she vses to seale" that convinces the steward Malvolio of the authenticity of the letter "to the unknowne belou'd," where the myth is evoked in the opening rhyme:

> *I may command where I adore, but silence like a Lucresse knife*
> *With bloodlesse stroke my heart doth gore.*
>
> (*TN*, 2.5.92–106)

The most striking command to the lover "no man must know" is "To see thee euer cross garter'd" (2.5.154). We noted before the possible relevance of Malvolio's cross-gartering to Shakespeare's attitude to the Garter ritual. Its association with the allusion to Lucrece confirms the surmise.

The presence of the myth of Lucrece persisted till the late romances, in the imaginary rape of Imogen by "yellow Iachimo" in *Cymbeline* (2.2.12–14):

> Our *Tarquine* thus
> Did softly presse the Rushes, ere he waken'd
> The Chastitie he wounded.

By this time the Roman myth had taken on a new significance. Already in the early poem Shakespeare had stressed the fact that Tarquin "hates himself for his offence," revealing his awareness of power as prevarication. *Edward III* marks the fusion of the Lucrece with the Garter myth, by showing a reformed Tarquin addressing his would-be victim with the words

> Arise, true English Ladie, whom our Ile
> May better boast of then euer Romaine might,
> Of her whose ransackt treasurie hath taskt,
> The vaine indeuor of so many pens.
>
> (988–91 [2.2])

The Garter Jig

The conceited comedy of *Sir John Falstaff and the Merry Wives of Windsor*—the jig concluding the Garter cycle that had presented in comic terms the sexual (but in fact political) prevarication of Henry V over Katherine of France—can be read as a parodic rendering of the story told in *The Reign of King Edward the third* of the "amours" that originated the most noble chivalric Order of England. Sir John Falstaff, "corrupt, and tainted in desire," like Edward in his infatuation for the Countess of Salisbury, is taught his lesson by the honest though merry wives whom he wanted to seduce, in the course of a celebration of the Order of the Garter. From history to parody, the parable of the Garter is complete.

Notes

Chapter 1. The Corridors of History: Shakespeare the Remaker

1. In the "Address to the Reader" in his *The English Traveller* (1633), Thomas Heywood claimed that he "had either an entire hand, or at least a maine finger" in no less than 220 plays.

2. Letter in *TLS*, 18 January 1985.

3. D. Bevington, *Tudor Drama and Politics* (Cambridge: Harvard University Press, 1968), 230ff.

4. Janet Clare, *"Art made tongue-tied by authority": Elizabethan and Jacobean Dramatic Censorship* (Manchester: Manchester University Press, 1990), 24–50.

5. On Anthony Munday's connection with Shakespeare see chapter 4, "Falstaff's Ancestry."

6. For the Revels Plays: *Sir Thomas More. A Play by Anthony Munday and Others Revised by Henry Chettle, Thomas Dekker, Thomas Heywood and William Shakespeare*, ed. Vittorio Gabrieli and Giorgio Melchiori (Manchester: Manchester University Press, 1990). My references here are to Greg's edition of *The Book of Sir Thomas More* (MSR, 1911); an asterisk (*) indicates lines after the first gap, and a dagger (†) after the second gap in the original manuscript.

7. My references, here and later, are to volume, page, and when necessary column and line, of the enlarged 1587 edition of Holinshed's *Chronicles* (abbr. *Hol.*); the words quoted here are from a marginal heading.

8. For an attempted conjectural reconstruction of the lost original version of the scene, see my paper "Hand D in *Sir Thomas More:* An Essay in Misinterpretation", *SSur.*, 38 (1985), 101–14.

9. John Strype, *Annals of the Reformation* (London, 1725–31), 4.168.

10. More, *Utopia* (Robinson's translation, 1551), sig. C7v.

11. See P. Maas, "Henry Finch and Shakespeare," *RES* n.s. 4 (1953), 142.

12. Scott McMillin, *The Elizabethan Theatre & "The Book of Sir Thomas More"* (Ithaca: Cornell University Press, 1987), agrees on 1593 as the date for this addition (though not for the others), whereas 1603 is strongly favored by Gary Taylor, "The date and auspices of the Additions to *Sir Thomas More*," in T. Howard-Hill, ed., *Shakespeare and "Sir Thomas More": Essays on the Play and its Shakespearean Interest* (Cambridge: Cambridge University Press, 1989), 101–21.

13. See the admirable edition by A. P. Rossiter, *Woodstock: A Moral History* (London: Chatto and Windus, 1946).

14. The famous anecdote about the box on the ear received by Tarlton as the lord chief justice during a performance of the play was reported in *Tarltons Ieasts*, entered in the Stationers' Register in 1609, but extant only in the 1638 edition.

15. John Dover Wilson's argument in "The Origins and Development of Shakespeare's 'Henry IV,'" 4 *Library*, 24 (1945), 9–11 (henceforward abbr. "Origins") that *Famous Victories* is an awkward conflation of two separate Queen's

Men's plays of different dates, which are the real sources of Shakespeare's remakes, does not prevent us from considering *FV* as Shakespeare's model, since the two plays are lost.

16. The description is from the Prologue of *The First Part of Sir John Oldcastle*, by Munday, Drayton, Wilson, and Hathway (1599); see P. Simpson's edition (MSR, 1908). A fully annotated modernized spelling edition of the play is found in *The Oldcastle Controversy*, ed. Peter Corbin and Douglas Sedge (the Revels Plays Companion Library, Manchester: Manchester University Press, 1991). Henceforward abbr. Corbin & Sedge.

17. *A Brief Chronicle concerning the Examination and Death of the Blessed Martyr of Christ, Sir John Oldcastle, the Lord Cobham* (1544). See Corbin & Sedge, 6–7 and 200–202.

18. See E. A. J. Honigmann, *Shakespeare: The Lost Years* (Manchester: Manchester University Press, 1985), *passim*.

19. *The life and death of Sir Thomas More, knight, sometymes Lord high Chancellor of England, written in the tyme of Queene Marie by Nicholas Harpsfield, L. D.*, ed. Elsie Vaughan Hitchcock (EETS, o.s. 186, 1932), 92–99. The relevant pages are reproduced in Appendix 2 to *The Second Part of King Henry IV*, ed. G. Melchiori (The New Cambridge Shakespeare, Cambridge: Cambridge University Press, 1989), 224–25.

20. See "A Defence of the Lord Cobham, Against Nicholas Harpsfield," in J. Foxe, *Acts and Monuments*, ed. J. Pratt (London, 1874), 3.348–402. Extracts from it are given in Corbin & Sedge, 203–15.

21. Act, scene, and line numbers in Shakespeare quotations, but not necessarily spelling and punctuation, are from *The Riverside Shakespeare*, ed. G. Blakemore Evans (Boston, 1974), even in the case of *2 Henry IV*, where in my edition (Cambridge, 1989) I have used different scene divisions. The usual abbreviations are used for Shakespeare's works.

22. This point will be discussed in chapter 3, à propos of the Epilogue of *2 Henry IV*, with reference to Alice-Lyle Scoufos's book, *Shakespeare's Typological Satire: A Study of the Falstaff-Oldcastle Problem* (Athens: Ohio University Press, 1979), esp. p.76f.

23. See the discussion of the ur-*Henry IV* in the next chapter.

24. For the opposite view see David Wiles, *Shakespeare's Clown: Actor and Text in the Elizabethan Playhouse* (Cambridge: Cambridge University Press, 1987), who devotes a whole chapter (116–35) to Falstaff, arguing that "Falstaff is structurally the clown's part," and that, therefore, it was written for William Kemp. I give the reasons for my view in discussing the Epilogue of *2H4*, chapter 3.

25. Wilson, "Origins."

26. E. M. W. Tillyard, *Shakespeare's History Plays* (London: Chatto and Windus, 1944), *passim*.

27. "'The Reign of King Edward III' (1596) and Shakespeare," *PBA*, 71 (1985), 159–85.

28. Gary Taylor, "The Fortunes of Oldcastle", *SSur.*, 38 (1985), 85–100.

29. This point is developed in the discussion of the Epilogue of *2H4* in my chapter 3.

30. Kristian Smidt, *Unconformities in Shakespeare's History Plays* (London: Macmillan, 1982); henceforward abbreviated *Unconformities*.

31. Chapter 2, "From Ur-Henry IV to Henriad."

32. Discussed in chapter 3.

33. They are given in chapter 6.

34. In his *The Structural Problem in Shakespeare's Henry IV* (London: Methuen, 1956).

35. Scene ix in the Praetorius facsimile edition of *Famous Victories*, introd. P. A. Daniel (London, 1887). The same scene numbering is adopted in the very useful annotated modern spelling edition in Corbin & Sedge, 145–99.

36. See in the next chapter a discussion of the reasons for the choice.

37. L. C. Knights, "Time's Subjects: The Sonnets and *King Henry IV, Part II,*" in his *Some Shakespearean Themes* (London: Chatto and Windus, 1959), 45–64.

38. Ibid., p. 63.

39. J. Joyce, *Ulysses*, "corrected text," ed. H. W. Gabler (New York: Garland, 1984), 69.

40. E. Hall, *The Union of the Two Noble and Illustre Fameliees of Lancastre and Yorke* (1548), as quoted in G. Bullough, ed., *Narrative and Dramatic Sources of Shakespeare*, 3 (London: Routledge and Kegan Paul, 1960), 17.

41. T. S. Eliot, *Collected Poems, 1909–1935* (London: Faber and Faber, 1936), 37–38.

42. In his study of the earlier use of the word ("'Policy,' Machiavellianism, and the Earlier Tudor Drama," *ELR*, 1 (1971), 195–209) Nigel Bawcutt rightly remarks that "the unfavourable connotations of 'policy' had so intensified by the end of the sixteenth century as to become perhaps the dominant implication of the word." In the present book as well as in *Shakespeare: politica e contesto economico* (Rome: Bulzoni, 1992) I try to show how Shakespeare's own policy, based on his awareness of the semantic complexity of the word, which he uses no less than forty-five times in his plays, consists in constantly playing on its ambiguity.

43. This opinion, widely shared by recent editors of the play (see *2 Henry IV*, ed. Melchiori), is repeated by Kristian Smidt, *Unconformities*, discussed more amply in the next chapter.

44. M. Spevack, *A Complete and Systematic Concordance to the Works of Shakespeare*, 9 vols. (Hildesheim: Georg Olms, 1968–80).

45. On Shakespeare's ambivalent attitude toward Prince Hal/Henry V, see Mary Axton, *The Queen's Two Bodies: Drama and the Elizabethan Succession* (London: Historical Society, 1977), 113–15.

46. Irving Ribner in *The English History Play in the Age of Shakespeare* (Princeton: Princeton University Press, 1957) lists some fifty history plays written before 1606 against only seventeen from that date to the middle of the seventeenth century.

47. M. Doran, "Iago's *If*—Conditional and Subjunctive in *Othello*," in her *Shakespeare's Dramatic Language* (Madison: Wisconsin University Press, 1976), 63–91; A. Serpieri, *Otello: L'Eros negato* (Milan: Formichiere, 1978).

Chapter 2. Reconstructing the Ur-*Henry IV*

1. *The Famous Victories of Henry the fifth: Containing the Honourable Battell of Agin-court: As it was plaide by the Queenes Maiesties Plaiers*. London. Printed by Thomas Creede, 1598. Abbr. *FV* in quotations. I adopt the scene divisions (in small Roman figures) and line numbering indicated in the margin of the Praetorius facsimile edition, introd. P. A. Daniel (London, 1887). They coincide with those of the modern spelling edition in Corbin & Sedge.

2. The idea of a one-play version of *Henry IV* was maintained by John Dover Wilson, "Origins," 2–16. Though later denied in favor of the view that either *Henry IV* was planned from the beginning as a two-part play, or that Shakespeare

changed his mind during its composition because of the excess of material, the one-play theory has been effectively revived by Kristian Smidt, *Unconformities,* through a study of the incongruities in the two Parts of the play, revealing the existence of a previous version.

3. Quotations in the following pages are from the first Quarto of *1 Henry IV,* published by Andrew Wise in 1598, and from the only Quarto of *2 Henry IV,* published by Andrew Wise and William Aspley in 1600; original signatures are indicated when necessary.

4. *Unconformities,* 111–15.

5. See the magnificent facsimile edition, *The History of King Henry the Fourth as revised by Sir Edward Dering, Bart.,* ed. G. Walton Williams and G. Blakemore Evans (Charlottesville, Folger Facsimiles, 1974); and for the date Laetitia Yeandle, "The dating of Sir Edward Dering's copy of 'The History of King Henry the Fourth'," *SQ,* 37 (1986), 224–26.

6. This is the 1623 Folio reading. The 1602 Quarto, a badly reported text, cuts the speech altogether.

7. Falstaff is supposed to "prick" four out of six recruits offered, but he actually takes three out of five; see *Unconformities,* 111–12 and n.25.

8. Stamford is the Folio reading, while Quarto has "Samforth," that some editors take to be a misreading of "Tamworth"; but the suggestion is untenable on palaeographical grounds.

9. A. E. Morgan, *Some Problems of Shakespeare's 'Henry the Fourth'* (London: Shakespeare Association paper, 1924), 40, lists five other cases in which Falstaff's name seems a last minute replacement for Oldcastle, or a belated addition, at 2.4.360, 365 (where "Falstaff, goodnight" seems an afterthought), 4.3.26, 5.2.33, and 5.5.91.

10. The full title is given him on the very first page (*sir Iohn Oldcastle,* sig. A2), but immediately afterward the stage direction reads *Enters Iockey;* in scene vi, though, he has the full title in the entrance direction (sig. C1), while throughout the text speech headings vary from *Iockey, Iock., Ioc.,* to *Ioh.Old.*

11. See *1 Henry IV,* 2.2.50–51 (sig. C3v): "O tis our setter, I know his voice."

12. The spelling of the surname varies a lot; Stokes, reported in M. A. Shaaber, ed., *The Second Part of Henry the Fourth* (New Variorum edition, Philadelphia and London: J. P. Lippincott, 1940), 4, speaks of "the family of Poyntz, one of high antiquity, in Gloucestershire."

13. A.-L. Scoufos, "Harvey: A Name Change in Henry IV", *ELH,* 36 (1961), 297–318, elaborated in her *Typological Satire,* chapter 8.

14. See *1 Henry VI,* 1.1.131, 1.4.35, 3.2. (whole scene), and 4.1.9–47, where Talbot plucks the Garter from "Sir John Falstaffe"'s leg.

15. Of course, Shakespeare used also other historical sources, but Holinshed, in the enlarged posthumous edition of 1587, is so obviously his main guide that I shall not mention Hall or Stow to avoid complicating the issue.

16. Variorum ed., 5.

17. G. Melchiori, "Sir John Umfrevile in *Henry IV,* Part 2, 1.1.161–79," *REAL* 2 (1984), 199–209.

18. This is a very different case from that of other plays set mainly from authorial foul papers, such as the 1599 Quarto of *Romeo and Juliet,* where the designation of one character changes from scene to scene according to the specific role of the character in each situation, so that, for instance, Lady Capulet is by turns "Mother," "Wife," "Lady," and even toward the end, "Old La."

19. I believe that Falstaff's pretense to be deaf to the Lord Chief Justice's servant (ll.65–91) is a piece of mere padding added during the writing of the

sequel, suggested by a passage that did appear in ur-*Henry IV*, on the nature of "appoplexi" (ll. 117–22; sig. B2v): " *Falst.* . . . it is a kind of deafenes. *Iust.* I think you are falne into the disease, for you heare not what I say to you. *Old.* Very wel my lord, very wel, rather and't please you—it is the disease of not listening the maladie of not marking that I am troubled withall." The heading *Old.* occurs exactly in this passage.

20. See R. B. McKerrow, "A Suggestion Regarding Shakespeare's Manuscripts," *RES* n.s. 11 (1935).

21. Smidt, *Unconformities*, 111.

22. The opening words of the soliloquy, "I know you all," are awkward, because only Poins was on stage and has just left; Herbert Weil suggests that they refer to the audience rather than the companions. Other inconsistencies are discussed by A. G. Gross, "The Text of Hal's First Soliloquy," *English Miscellany*, 18 (1969), 49–54, and cf. *Unconformities*, 107–8 and n. 10.

23. This instance should be added to Morgan's list *(Some Problems)* reported in note 9.

24. Modern editions include also the "setter" Gadshill among those present because in the Folio (sig. e4) the speech headings *Ross.* are changed into *Gad.* In fact, Gadshill has no other speeches and is never addressed during the scene, and there are no specific entrance or exit directions either for him or for Falstaff's other companions. I take it that the reviser of the copy for the Folio, faced with the survival of the speech heading *Ross.* (which he did not know stood for the name originally given to Bardolph) replaced it with the name of the only participant in the Gad's Hill robbery who had no speech in the current scene; but Shakespeare, both in ur-*Henry IV* and in the rewritten play, never meant this menial figure to be present at the revelation of the trick played by the Prince and Pointz on their companions. For a more elaborate view of the case see J. Jowett, "The Thieves in *1 Henry IV*", *RES* n.s. 38 (1987), 325–33.

25. This has been noticed by Smidt, *Unconformities*, 112–13.

26. S. H. Hawkins, in "*Henry IV:* The Structural Problem Revisited," *SQ,* 33 (1982), 281, maintains that the scene "is fatal to the notion of Part 2 as an unpremeditated addition"; but he overlooks the previous mentions of the Archbishop's role in Part One, and has to acknowledge that he is mentioned by Holinshed as helping the rebels *before* Shrewsbury.

27. John Jowett and Gary Taylor, "The Three Texts of *2 Henry IV*", *SB*, 40 (1987), 31–50, demonstrate how the scene could have been written on a separate leaf not included in the first issue of the 1600 Quarto; but I cannot agree with them that this scene as well as eight more long passages missing from both issues of Quarto should be considered not as omissions but as additions to the text, written somewhat later.

28. Morgan, *Some Problems*, and Wilson, "Origins."

29. The significance of the presence of the figures of carnival in *Henry IV* is illustrated by Leonard Tennenhouse, *Power on Display: The Politics of Shakespeare's Genres* (London: Methuen, 1986), esp. 83–84.

Chapter 3. From Ur-*Henry IV* to Henriad: Rewriting as Subversion

1. Stephen Greenblatt, "Invisible Bullets: Renaissance authority and Its Subversion, *Henry IV* and *Henry V*," *Political Shakespeare: New Essays in Cultural Materialism*, ed. John Dollimore and Alan Sinfield (Manchester: Manchester University

Press, 1985), 18–47, later included in his *Shakespearean Negotiations* (1987). Parts of the article appeared in 1981.

2. See E. A. Strathmann, *Sir Walter Ralegh* (New York: Columbia University Press, 1951). Recent editions of *Love's Labour's Lost,* including that by G. R. Hibbard (Oxford: Oxford University Press, 1990), tend to discredit the reading "school of night" in the play (4.3.251) as an ironical allusion to Ralegh's circle. In *The Complete Works,* ed. S. Wells and G. Taylor with J. Jowett and W. Montgomery (Oxford: Clarendon Press, 1986), Stanley Wells emends to "style of night"; see his argument in *A Textual Companion* (Oxford: Clarendon Press, 1987), 274.

3. The following paragraph is from my introduction to the New Cambridge Shakespeare *2 Henry IV,* 30.

4. Reported in *Tarlton's Jests,* see note 14 to chapter 1.

5. *R2,* 1.1.76; cf. Richard C. McCoy, *The Rites of Knighthood: The Literature and Politics of Elizabethan Knighthood* (Berkeley and Los Angeles: University of California Press, 1989), introduction, 1.

6. *2H4,* 2.1.136–65.

7. On the relevance to the creation of Falstaff of the Grant of Arms see "Fastolf and Falstaff versus Oldcastle," in chapter 5.

8. See "A galaxy of garters," chapter 6.

9. Here is a list based on the reconstruction of the early play in the previous chapter. Historical: 3.1 (the night musings of the king); 4.4 and 4.5 (the deathbed scenes—with the insertion of new material); 5.2 (the confirmation of the Lord Chief Justice); 5.5.79–108 (final comments of Prince John and Justice). Comic: 1.2.92–174ca (a single page from the meeting of Falstaff and the Lord Chief Justice); 2.1.133–35 and 166–95 (echoes of a conversation between the Lord Chief Justice and a messenger); 2.2.1–64ca (single page of a conversation between the Prince and Poins); 2.4.354–65 (the summons to court); 3.2 (the enrollment scene) may contain echoes of a much shorter scene in ur-*Henry IV;* 5.5.43–72 (the rejection of Falstaff).

10. John Dover Wilson, *The Fortunes of Falstaff* (Cambridge: Cambridge University Press, 1953), 14ff.

11. See for instance John Redford's *Wit and Science* (1535–45ca), Richard Wever's *Lusty Juventus* (1560ca), *The Trial of Treasure* (1567), Thomas Ingelend's *The Disobedient Child* (1569ca), *The Marriage of Wit and Science* (1570), and Francis Merbury's *Marriage of Wit and Wisdom* (1579).

12. The best-known example is John Bale's *King Johan,* where, for instance, an exit stage direction instructs the actors taking the roles of Usurped Power, Private Wealth, and Sedition, to change into the costumes of the Pope, Cardinal Pandulphus, and Archbishop Steven Langton respectively. See J. H. Pafford and W. W. Greg, eds., *King Johan* (MSR, 1931), line 1002: "her go owt usurpid powr & privat welth and sedycyon: usurpyd powr shall drese for the pope: privat welth for a cardynall and sedytyon for stevyn launton a monke." Cf my "Peter, Balthasar, and Shakespeare's Art of Doubling," *MLR* 78 (1983), 777–92.

13. The lines are part of one of the eight passages of the play found only in the Folio version—hence, the extensive use of capitalization, which is instead used very sparingly by the printers of the Quarto. The echo in them of Induction, 16, is further confirmation that those passages were not later additions to the text, but parts of the original script omitted in the printing of the 1600 Quarto for theatrical or political reasons. See "Textual analysis" in the New Cambridge edition of the play (Melchiori, 1989), 189–202.

14. Variorum, 13. It is odd that the strongest advocate of the superiority of the Quarto over the Folio text so far, Eleanor Prosser, in her extremely thorough

study of the text of the play, *Shakespeare's Anonymous Editors: Scribe and Compositor in the Folio Text of 2 Henry IV* (Stanford: Stanford University Press, 1981), although castigating recent editors for having rejected Q readings in no less than eighty instances, completely ignores this case, which would have added further supporting evidence to her argument.

15. William Montgomery in *Complete Works* (Oxford, 1986), 575; Melchiori in *2 Henry IV* (Cambridge, 1989), 60. The new reading was adopted after the publication of T. L. Berger and G. W. Williams, "Notes on Shakespeare's *2 Henry IV*," *AEB* 3 (1979), 241, and of a note of mine in *SQ* 34 (1983), 327–30.

16. A study of the text shows that, apart from proper names and geographical or topographical designations ("Orient," "the sign of the Legge" for the name of a tavern), capitals are reserved for titles, whether noble, military, or professional (including "Tapster," "Car-men," "Berod" [bearherd], "Tennis court keeper"), for abusive and jocular nouns ("Cunger," "Cracke," "Besonian"), for texts ("Anthem," "Almanacke"), and for collective nouns ("Chevalry," "Sneakes Noise").

17. For example, those of cardinal points: "Orient," "West," line 3.

18. *The First Part of Sir John Oldcastle*, ed. P. Simpson (MSR, 1908). The point is discussed in Corbin and Sedge, who include also ample extracts of the poem written with the same object by John Weever, *The Mirror of Martyrs, or, The life and death of that thrice valiant Captain and most godly Martyr Sir John Oldcastle Knight, Lord Cobham* (1601, but composed in 1599).

19. No longer in Eastcheap. For the location of Mistress Quickly's (now Pistol's wife) establishment see "The dual chronology of the Falstaff plays," postscript to chapter 5.

20. Variorum, 460.

21. *The Second Part of the History of Henry IV*, ed. J. Dover Wilson (Cambridge: Cambridge University Press, 1946), 215; *The Second Part of King Henry IV*, ed. A. R. Humphreys (New Arden Shakespeare, London: Methuen, 1966), 187. Cf. A. A. Mendilow, "Falstaff's Death of a Sweat," *SQ* 9 (1958), 479–83, and the ironic figurative use of the dreaded lethal illness in Thomas Nashe's *Unfortunte Traveller* (1594): "Let me . . . tell a little of the sweating sicknes, that made me in a cold sweate take my heeles and runne out of England." (Quoted in *OED*, s.v. Sweating-sickness).

22. Scoufos, *Typological Satire*, 76–77.

23. The name change in this line was first pointed out by Joseph Ritson in 1793, see *Henry the Fourth Part I*, ed. S. B. Hemingway (New Variorum edition, Philadelphia: J. P. Lipincott, 1936), 450.

24. See chapter 5. The misapprehension may be summarized in the words of a "young gentle lady" who candidly asked the librarian Dr. Richard James (as he reports in an epistle to Sir Henry Bourchier) how Falstaff, banished for cowardice under Henry VI, could have died at the time of Henry V. I give there my reasons for believing that the confusion in the names is deliberate and not the result of compositorial interference or casual homonimy.

Chapter 4. Falstaff's Ancestry: From Verona to Windsor

1. See chapter 5.
2. See the references to these two comedies in chapter 6.
3. See "The role of policy"in chapter 1.
4. Leo Salingar, *Shakespeare and the Traditions of Comedy* (Cambridge: Cambridge University Press, 1974), "Shakespeare and Italian Comedy," 175–242.

Cf. Louise George Clubb, *Italian Drama in Shakespeare's Time* (New Haven: Yale University Press, 1989).

5. Salingar, *Traditions*, 228–38.

6. Jeanne Addison Roberts, *Shakespeare's English Comedy:* The Merry Wives of Windsor *in Context* (Lincoln: University of Nebraska Press, 1979), Introduction, xvi.

7. See for instance Alexander Leggatt, *Citizen Comedy in the Age of Shakespeare* (Toronto: Toronto University Press, 1973).

8. Clubb, *Italian Drama*, 25–26.

9. For a general view of the origins and fortune of romance on the Elizabethan and Jacobean stage, see my paper "Romance into Drama," in *Atti del V Congresso Nazionale dell'Associazione Italiana di Anglistica*, ed. M. P. De Angelis, V. Fortunati and V. Poggi (Bologna: Clueb, 1983), 15–29.

10. *Fidele and Fortunio The Two Italian Gentlemen*, ed. Percy Simpson (MSR, 1910 for 1909).

11. *The Downfall of the Earl of Huntington* and *The Death of the Earl of Huntington*, mentioned in connection with theatrical "sequels" in chapter 1.

12. On the career of Anthony Munday see Celeste Turner, *Anthony Mundy: An Elizabethan Man of Letters* (University of California Publications in English), vol. 2, no. 1 (1928).

13. Shakespeare's intervention (as Hand D) in *The Book of Sir Thomas More* is discussed in chapter 1.

14. In the Prologue to *The First Part of Sir John Oldcastle*, referred to in the discussion of the Epilogue of *2H4*, chapter 3.

15. Clubb, 50, in a footnote mentions it in a list of such translations: "Pasqualigo's *Il Fedele* in Fraunce's Latin *Victoria* and Munday's *Fedele and Fortunio, the two Italian Gentlemen*."

16. Salingar, *Traditions*, 189.

17. He claimed that he went there with the deliberate intention of reporting on his fellow students, refugee English Catholics considered guilty of high treason.

18. G. C. Moore-Smith, ed. *Materialen zur Kunde des älteren englischen Dramas*, vol. 14, Louvain, 1906.

19. All references are to Richard Hosley, ed., *A Critical Edition of Anthony Munday's Fedele and Fortunio* (New York: Garland, 1981); I have modernized the spelling. Hosley's introduction includes parallel summaries of the English and Italian texts, emphasizing the transformation undergone by *Il Fedele* in Munday's version.

20. In the later French adaptation of *Il Fedele* by Pierre Larivey (*Le Fidelle*, 1611), Frangipietra's name is translated "Brisemur" (Crackwall); see Daniel C. Boughner, *The Braggart in Renaissance Comedy: A Study in Comparative Drama from Aristophanes to Shakespeare* (Minneapolis: University of Minnesota Press, 1954), 264–65.

21. Salingar, *Traditions*, 232.

22. Boughner, *Braggart*, 88. Boughner had not seen Munday's adaptation of *Il Fedele*.

23. A. Quiller-Couch and J. Dover Wilson, eds., *The Merry Wives of Windsor* (Cambridge: Cambridge University Press, 1921), Introduction, xxii.

24. "The Italianate Background of *The Merry Wives of Windsor*," *University of Michigan Publications in Language and Literature*, 8 (1932): 81–117.

Chapter 5. Reconstructing the Garter Entertainment at Westminster on St. George's Day 23 April 1597

1. William Green, *Shakespeare's Merry Wives of Windsor* (Princeton: Princeton University Press, 1962). Roberts, *English Comedy*, already mentioned, is a more recent study along the same lines.

2. This appears from Armin's own play, *The Two Maids of More-Clacke,* **see** A. S. Liddie's introduction to his critical edition of the play (New York: Garland, 1979). Armin reserved for himself in it the part of a comic Welshman as well as that of the clown. The language of Owen Glendower in *1 Henry IV*, written before Armin's advent, counts for comic effect on its grandiloquence, but it shows no trace of the equivocations caused by the Welsh accent, which character- ize instead Fluellen and Sir Hugh Evans.

3. The curious intervention of Bardolph in the extremely brief scene 4.3, and the inconsequential scene (4.5.60–86) when the Host of the Garter is in- formed that three Germans have stolen his horses under pretense of needing them to meet a duke, has been taken to allude to a German nobleman who, when visiting England in 1592 as Frederick Count Mömpelgard, had maneuvred to be elected to the Order of the Garter, but when, having become Duke of Württemberg, the honor was conferred upon him in 1597, did not attend the installation ceremony. William Green (121–76) devotes a whole chapter to "The Duke of Jarmany."

4. G. Hibbard, ed. *The Merry Wives of Windsor* (New Penguin Shakespeare, Harmondsworth: Penguin Books, 1973), introduction 49–50.

5. A reference to Dennis's statement that the comedy was written in a fort- night at the Queen's command, quoted in "The Garter Comedy" section of chapter 4.

6. On the Elizabethan cult of chastity see Philippa Berry, *Of Chastity and Power* (London: Routledge, 1989).

7. Anne Barton, introducing *The Merry Wives of Windsor* in The Riverside Shakespeare, ed. G. Blakemore Evans (Boston: Houghton Mifflin, 1974), 286, remarks that "a comedy concerned, as this one is, with the punishment of a knight whose principles and behaviour contravene all the ideals of his rank would be appropriate, almost as a kind of antimasque, at a Garter feast."

8. The two lines of the couplet (80 and 83) were spoken alternately by Satyr and Hobgoblin (Folio, p.51, sig. E6):

[*Evan.*] But stay, I smell a man of middle earth.
Pist. Vilde worme, thou wast ore-look'd euen in thy birth.

9. Quotations of *1 Henry VI*, here and in the next chapter, are from the First Folio of 1623, Histories, 110, sig. 13v.

10. See chapter 3, note 24. Taylor ("Fortunes") believes that the epistle was written in 1634 rather than about 1625, the date commonly accepted.

11. Quoted by Taylor, "Fortunes," 86.

12. *The First Part of King Henry VI*, ed. Michael Hattaway (New Cambridge Shakespeare. Cambridge: Cambridge University Press, 1991), 64.

13. George Walton Williams, "Fastolf or Falstaff," *ELR,* 5 (1975), 308–12; Robert F. Willson, Jr, "Falstaff in *Henry IV:* What's in a Name?" *SQ,* 27 (1976), 199–200; Norman Davis, "Falstaff's Name," *SQ,* 28 (1977), 513–15; G. W. Wil- liams, "Second Thoughts on Falstaff's Name," *SQ,* 30 (1979), 82–84.

14. E. K. Chambers, *William Shakespeare: A Study of Facts and Problems* (Oxford:

Clarendon Press, 1930), 2. 27, and 2.371–75 ("Spelling and Significance of the Name").

15. T. Walter Herbert, "The Naming of Falstaff," *Emory University Quarterly*, 10 (March 1954), 1–11; Harry Levin, "Shakespeare's Nomenclature." *Essays on Shakespeare*, ed. G. W. Chapman (Princeton: Princeton University Press, 1965), 87.

16. Roberts, *English Comedy*, 48.

17. Chambers, *Shakespeare*, 2.18–32.

18. See chapter 1, "The Corridors of History: Shakespeare the Remaker." and chapter 2, "Reconstructing the Ur-*Henry IV*," in this book.

19. A likely jocular reference to the new genre of the comedy of humors, established by Ben Jonson's *Every Man in His Humour*, a play presented on the stage between July and September 1598, with Shakespeare as one in the cast. See the postscript to the present chapter.

20. *The Merry Wives of Windsor*, ed. J. H. Oliver (New Arden Shakespeare, London: Methuen, 1971).

21. *The Merry Wives of Windsor*, ed. T. W. Craik (Oxford: Oxford University Press, 1990).

22. Roberts, *English Comedy*, 38–40.

23. E.J. A. Honigmann, "Sir John Oldcastle: Shakespeare's Martyr," in J. W. Mahon and T. A. Pendleton, eds., *"Fanned and Winnowed Opinions" Shakespearean Essays Presented to Harold Jenkins* (London: Methuen, 1987), 118–32.

24. The exchange is practically identical in the earlier version of the play, the 1602 Quarto (sig. B1v), except for Bardolph's last speech that reads: "I will sir, Ile warrant you Ile make a good shift to liue."

25. In 1602 Quarto, sig.F3: "Syr heere be three Gentlemen come from the Duke the St[r]anger sir, would haue your horse."

26. 1602 Quarto: "Ile call them to you sir."

27. 1602 Quarto: "House."

28. Roberts, *English Comedy*, 41–50.

29. 1986, text of the play edited by John Jowett, checked by Gary Taylor.

30. Roberts, *English Comedy*, 45.

31. *Textual Companion*, 1987, 120.

32. Roberts, *English Comedy*, 46.

33. Green, *Merry Wives*, 88–92.

34. Green, *Merry Wives*, 190–92.

35. *Henry V*, ed. Gary Taylor (Oxford: Oxford University Press, 1982), 63–64.

Chapter 6. Five Falstaffs and the Countess of Salisbury: *Edward III* as a Garter Play

1. *R3*, 4.4.366ff, quoted in chapter 3.

2. I am deliberately ignoring the "garters" (or "straps") mentioned in connection with the proverbial saying "He may go hang himself in his own garters" (M. P. Tilley, *A Dictionary of Proverbs in England* [Ann Arbor: University of Michigan Press, 1950]; item G42) in *A Midsummer Night's Dream*, 5.1.357–60, and *Twelfth Night*, 1.3.12–13; though the variant adopted by Falstaff in addressing Prince Hal in *1 Henry IV* (2.2.43–44), "Hang thyself in thine own heir-apparent garters," is undoubtedly significant.

3. Peter Erickson, "The Order of the Garter, the Cult of Elizabeth, and Class-Gender Tension in *The Merry Wives of Windsor*," in *Shakespeare Reproduced*.

The Text in History and Ideology, ed. Jean E. Howard and Marion F. O'Connor (London: Methuen 1987), 116–40.

4. Erickson, "Garter," 127. The quotation in inverted commas is from Juliet Vale, *Edward III and Chivalry: Chivalric Society and its Context, 1270–1350* (Woodbridge: Boydell Press, 1982), 87.

5. Polydore Vergil, *Historia Anglica* (1555), Scolar Press facsimile (Menston: Scolar Press, 1970), lib.XIX, pp. 378–79. The quotation from Holinshed is from the second edition of *Chronicles* (1587), 2. 366/2/44–69. The report of the death of the Earl of Salisbury is not in Polydore Vergil: a marginal note in Holinshed attributes it to "Additions to *Adam Merimuth* and *Triuet.*"

6. See especially Proudfoot, quoted in chapter 1, note 27. E. Slater, *The Problem of "The Reign of King Edward III": A Statistical Approach* (Cambridge: Cambridge University Press, 1988), concludes his sophisticated analysis of rare words and word links in *Edward III* with other plays by Shakespeare and contemporary authors by stating that (p.135) "it is compatible with authorship by Shakespeare at an early stage in his dramatic career. Both part A [1.2, the whole of Act 2 and 4.4] and part B [the rest of the play] are regarded as his work, though probably written at different times."

7. E. K. Chambers, *The Elizabethan Stage* (London: Oxford University Press, 1951), 1.322.

8. Line numbering (and occasional indications of act and scene) from *The Raigne of King Edward the Third,* A Critical, Old-Spelling Edition by Fred Lapides (New York: Garland, 1980).

9. It is significant that, although in most cases of new editions of plays previously published, the name of the company owning the play at the time of publication is mentioned in the title page, the 1599 Quarto of *Edward III* reproduces with only slight changes in spelling the noncommittal statement in the title page of the 1596 Quarto: "As it hath been Sundry times played about the Citie of London." It suggests that no company could for the time being stage the play or claim their right in it.

10. Frances A. Yates, *Astraea: The Imperial Theme in the Sixteenth Century* (London: Routledge, 1975) is the most comprehensive treatment of the subject. See especially pp. 108–12 on the Garter and Elizabethan chivalry.

11. McCoy, *Rites,* 20.

12. D. H. Horne, ed. *The Life and Minor Works of George Peele* (New Haven: Yale University Press, 1952), I:173–77; text 245–59.

13. Yates, *Astraea,* 60–62, points out the importance of Peele's 1591 City pageant *Descensus Astraeae* in shaping the myth of the virgin queen as Astraea.

14. Berry, *Chastity,* does not mention Peele's poem but elaborates (p. 143) on the allusion in *A Midsummer Night's Dream.*

15. Thomas Nashe, *Pierce Pennilesse his Supplication to the Diuell* (1592), Scolar Press facsimile (Menston: the Scolar Press, 1969), fol.26r, sig.H2.

16. See R. Prior, "The Date of *Edward III*," *Notes and Queries,* 235 (1990). For an ample survey and discussion of the date, authorship, and sources of the play see *Sources of Four Plays Ascribed to Shakespeare,* ed. and intro. G. Harold Metz (Columbia: Missouri University Press, 1989), 3–42 (henceforward "Metz, Sources").

17. Jean Froissart, *The Cronycle of Syr John Froissart. Translated out of French by Sir John Bourchier Lord Berners, annis 1523–25,* Edited by William Paton Ker, 6 vols. (London: David Nutt, 1901–3). The quotation is from chapter lxxvi (misnumbered lxxx in the 1525 ed.) of Books III–IV (Ker, 4.429). A detailed account of the battle of Najera, won by the Black Prince in 1367, is contained in chapters

ccxxxvii–ccxxxviii of Book II (Ker, 2.204–18). In the case of quotations of passages from Froissart reproduced in Metz, *Sources,* page references are to the latter.

18. J. Viard et E. Déprez ed., *Chronique de Jean le Bel,* (Paris: Société de l'histoire de France, 1904–5), II.30–34, ch. lxv. See also Antonia Gransden, "The alleged rape by Edward III of the countess of Salisbury," *English Historical Review,* 87 (1972): 333–44.

19. Le Bel, II.1–2, chap. lxi.

20. Le Bel, II.31.

21. *Chroniques de J. Froissart publiées pour la Société de l'Histoire de France par Simeon Luce.* Tome troisiéme, 1342–1346. Variantes du chapitre LIV (Paris: Renouard, 1872), 293.

22. Metz, *Sources,* 67 (b.I, ch. lxxvii).

23. Metz, *Sources,* 67 (b.1, ch. lxxxix).

24. Ibid., 68.

25. *The Cronycle of Froissart,* facsimile reprint (Amsterdam, 1970), Book I, chap. C (cf. Ker, 2.232–33). Though Holinshed agrees on 1344 as the date of the founding of the Order, other historians suggest the year 1347.

26. William Painter, *The Palace of Pleasure,* a reprint of the 1890 J. Jacobs edition (New York: Dover, 1966), 1.334–63.

27. Painter, *Palace of Pleasure,* 1.336.

28. See R. L. Armstrong's introduction to his edition of the play in *Six Early Plays Related to the Shakespeare Canon,* ed. E. B. Everitt, *Anglistica,* 14 (1963): 195–99.

29. It is the episode of the safeconduct granted by Prince Charles of Normandy to an English nobleman (Froissart/Berners, I.cxxxv), referred to later in this chapter ("Chivalry"). In Froissart, the Englishman is not the Earl of Salisbury but Sir Walter de Manny.

30. Painter, *Palace of Pleasure,* I.346.

31. G. Melchiori, *Shakespeare's Dramatic Meditations: An Experiment in Criticism* (Oxford: Clarendon Press, 1976), 42–67.

32. Tillyard, *History Plays,* 113–14.

33. M. C. Bradbrook, *The Living Monument* (Cambridge: Cambridge University Press, 1976), 230–32.

34. See "The role of policy," in chapter 1.

35. Holinshed, quoted in the section "The founding of the Order."

36. Ted Hughes, *Shakespeare and the Goddess of Complete Being* (London: Faber, 1992).

Works Cited

Anonymous. *The Famous Victories of Henry the fifth: Containing the Honourable Battell of Agin-court: As it was plaide by the Queenes Maiesties Plaiers. London: Printed by Thomas Creede, 1598.* A facsimile with an introduction by P. A. Daniel. London: Charles Praetorius, 1887.

Armin, Robert. *The Two Maids of More-Clacke.* 1607. A critical edition by A. S. Liddie. New York: Garland, 1979.

Armstrong, R. L., ed. *Edward III.* In *Six Early Plays Related to the Shakespeare Canon.* Edited by E. B. Everitt. *Anglistica* (Copenhagen: Rosenkilde and Banger, 1963) 14: 195–250.

Axton, Mary. *The Queen's Two Bodies: Drama and the Elizabethan Succession.* London: Historical Society, 1977.

Bale, John. *King Johan.* 1538ca. Edited by J. H. Pafford and W. W. Greg. Oxford: Malone Society Reprints, 1931.

———. *A Brief Chronicle concerning the Examination and Death of the Blessed Martyr of Christ, Sir John Oldcastle, the Lord Cobham.* In *The Oldcastle Controversy.* Edited by Peter Corbin and Douglas Sedge, 200–202. Manchester: Manchester University Press, 1991.

Bawcutt, Nigel. "'Policy,' Machiavellianism, and the Earlier Tudor Drama." *English Literary Renaissance* 1 (1971): 195–209.

Berger, T. L., and G. W. Williams. "Notes on Shakespeare's *2 Henry IV.*" *Analytical and Enumerative Bibliography* 3 (1979): 240–53.

Berry, Philippa. *Of Chastity and Power.* London: Routledge, 1989.

Bevington, David. *Tudor Drama and Politics.* Cambridge: Harvard University Press, 1968.

Boughner, Daniel C. *The Braggart in Renaissance Comedy: A Study in Comparative Drama from Aristophanes to Shakespeare.* Minneapolis: University of Minnesota Press, 1954.

Bradbrook, Muriel C. *The Living Monument.* Cambridge: Cambridge University Press, 1976.

Bullough, Geoffrey, ed. *Narrative and Dramatic Sources of Shakespeare.* 8 vols. London: Routledge and Kegan Paul, 1957–75.

Campbell, Oscar. "The Italianate Background of *The Merry Wives of Windsor.*" *University of Michigan Publications in Language and Literature* 8 (1932): 81–117.

Chambers, E. K. *William Shakespeare: A Study of Facts and Problems.* 2 vols. Oxford: Clarendon Press, 1930.

———. *The Elizabethan Stage.* 4 vols. London: Oxford University Press, 1951.

Clare, Janet. *"Art made Tongue-tied by Authority": Elizabethan and Jacobean Dramatic Censorship.* Manchester: Manchester University Press, 1990.

Clubb, Louise George. *Italian Drama in Shakespeare's Time.* New Haven: Yale University Press, 1989.

Corbin, Peter, and Douglas Sedge, eds. *The Oldcastle Controversy* (The Revels Plays Companion Library). Manchester: Manchester University Press, 1991.

Craik, T. W., ed. *The Merry Wives of Windsor.* Oxford: Oxford University Press, 1990.

Davis, Norman. "Falstaff's Name." *Shakespeare Quarterly* 28 (1977): 513–15.

Doran, Madeleine. "Iago's *If*— Conditional and Subjunctive in *Othello.*" In her *Shakespeare's Dramatic Language,* 63–91. Madison: Wisconsin University Press, 1976.

Eliot, T. S. *Collected Poems, 1909–1935.* London: Faber and Faber, 1936.

Erickson, Peter. "The Order of the Garter, the Cult of Elizabeth, and Class-Gender Tension in *The Merry Wives of Windsor.*" In Howard, Jean E. and Marion F. O'Connor, eds. *Shakespeare Reproduced. The Text in History and Ideology,* 116–40. London: Methuen, 1987.

Evans, G. Blakemore, ed. *The Riverside Shakespeare.* Boston: Houghton Mifflin, 1974.

Foxe, John. *The Ecclesiastical Historie, containing the Acts and Monuments of Martyrs.* 1583. Edited by J. Pratt. London: 1874.

Froissart, Jean. *The Cronycle of Syr John Froissart.* 6 vols. Translated out of French by Sir John Bourchier Lord Berners, annis 1523–25, Edited by William Paton Ker. London: David Nutt, 1901–3.

———. *The Cronycle of Froissart.* 1523–25. Facsimile reprint. Amsterdam, 1970.

———. *Chroniques de J. Froissart publiées pour la Société de l'Histoire de France par Simeon Luce.* Tomes 1–5, 1307–1360. Paris: Renouard, 1869–74.

Gabrieli, Vittorio, and Giorgio Melchiori, eds. *Sir Thomas More. A Play by Anthony Munday and Others, Revised by Henry Chettle, Thomas Dekker, Thomas Heywood and William Shakespeare* (The Revels Plays). Manchester: Manchester University Press, 1990.

Gransden, Antonia. "The Alleged Rape by Edward III of the Countess of Salisbury." *English Historical Review* 87 (1972): 333–44.

Green, William. *Shakespeare's Merry Wives of Windsor.* Princeton: Princeton University Press, 1962.

Greenblatt, Stephen. "Invisible bullets: Renaissance Authority and Its Subversion, *Henry IV* and *Henry V.*" In *Political Shakespeare: New Essays in Cultural Materialism.* Edited by John Dollimore and Alan Sinfield, 18–47. Manchester: Manchester University Press, 1985.

Greg, W. W., ed. *The Book of Sir Thomas More.* Oxford: Malone Society Reprints, 1911.

Gross, A. G. "The Text of Hal's First Soliloquy." *English Miscellany* 18 (1969): 49–54.

Harpsfield, Nicholas. *The life and death of Sir Thomas More, knight, sometymes Lord high Chancellor of England, written in the tyme of Queene Marie by Nicholas Harpsfield, L.D.* 1555 ca. Edited by Elsie Vaughan Hitchcock. Early English Texts Society. Old Series 186, 1932.

Hattaway, Michael, ed. *The First Part of King Henry VI.* The New Cambridge Shakespeare. Cambridge: Cambridge University Press, 1991.

Hawkins, S. H. *"Henry IV:* The Structural Problem Revisited." *Shakespeare Quarterly* 33 (1982): 279–301.

Hemingway, S. B., ed. *Henry the Fourth Part I.* New Variorum Edition. Philadelphia: J. P. Lippincott, 1936.

Herbert, T. Walter. "The Naming of Falstaff." *Emory University Quarterly* 10 (1954): 1–11.

Hibbard, G. R., ed. *The Merry Wives of Windsor.* New Penguin Shakespeare. Harmondsworth: Penguin Books, 1973.

———, ed. *Love's Labour's Lost.* Oxford: Oxford University Press, 1990.

Holinshed, Raphael. *The Chronicles of England, Scotland and Ireland . . . Now newly recognized, augmented, and continued . . . to the yeare 1586.* London, 1587.

Honigmann, E. A. J. *Shakespeare: The Lost Years.* Manchester: Manchester University Press, 1985.

———. "Sir John Oldcastle: Shakespeare's Martyr." In *"Fanned and Winnowed Opinions" Shakespearean Essays Presented to Harold Jenkins.* Edited by J. W. Mahon and T. A. Pendleton, 118–32. London: Methuen, 1987.

Horne, D. H., ed. *The Life and Minor Works of George Peele.* New Haven: Yale University Press, 1952.

Howard-Hill, T. H. ed. *Shakespeare and "Sir Thomas More": Essays on the Play and Its Shakespearean Interest.* Cambridge: Cambridge University Press, 1989.

Hughes, Ted. *Shakespeare and the Goddess of Complete Being.* London: Faber, 1992.

Humphreys, A. R., ed. *The Second Part of King Henry IV.* New Arden Shakespeare. London: Methuen, 1966.

Jenkins, Harold. *The Structural Problem in Shakespeare's Henry IV.* London: Methuen, 1956.

Jowett, John. "The Thieves in *1 Henry IV.*" *Review of English Studies* New Series 38 (1987): 325–33.

Jowett, John, and Gary Taylor. "The Three Texts of *2 Henry IV.*" *Studies in Bibliography* 40 (1987): 31–50.

Joyce, James. *Ulysses.* 1922. "Corrected Text." Edited by H. W. Gabler. New York: Garland, 1984.

Knights, Lionel C. "Time's Subjects: The Sonnets and *King Henry IV, Part II.*" In his *Some Shakespearean Themes,* 45–64. London: Chatto and Windus, 1959.

Lapides, Fred, ed., *The Raigne of King Edward the Third.* A Critical, Old-Spelling Edition. New York: Garland, 1980.

Le Bel, Jean. *Chronique de Jean le Bel,* 2 vols. Edited by J. Viard et E. Déprez. Paris: Société de l'histoire de France, 1924–5.

Leggatt, Alexander. *Citizen Comedy in the Age of Shakespeare.* Toronto: Toronto University Press, 1973.

Levin, Harry. "Shakespeare's Nomenclature." In *Essays on Shakespeare,* edited by G. W. Chapman. Princeton: Princeton University Press, 1965.

Maas, P. "Henry Finch and Shakespeare." *Review of English Studies* New Series 4 (1953): 142.

McCoy, Richard C. *The Rites of Knighthood: The Literature and Politics of Elizabethan Knighthood.* Berkeley and Los Angeles: University of California Press, 1989.

McKerrow, R. B. "A Suggestion Regarding Shakespeare's Manuscripts." *Review of English Studies* New Series 11 (1935): 459–65.

McMillin, Scott. *The Elizabethan Theatre & "The Book of Sir Thomas More."* Ithaca: Cornell Unviersity Press, 1987.

Melchiori, Giorgio. *Shakespeare's Dramatic Meditations: An Experiment in Criticism.* Oxford: Clarendon Press, 1976.

———. "Peter, Balthasar, and Shakespeare's Art of Doubling." *Modern Language Review* 78 (1983): 777–92.

———. "The Role of Jealousy: Restoring the Quarto Reading of *2 Henry IV*, Ind. 16." *Shakespeare Quarterly* 34 (1983): 327–30.

———. "Romance into Drama." In *Atti del V Congresso Nazionale dell'Associazione Italiana di Anglistica,* edited by M. P. De Angelis, V. Fortunati, and V. Poggi, 15–29. Bologna: CLUEB, 1983.

———. "Sir John Umfrevile in *Henry IV, Part 2*, 1.1.161–79." *REAL Yearbook of Research in English and American Studies* 2 (1984): 199–209.

———. "Hand D in Sir Thomas More: An Essay in Misinterpretation." *Shakespeare Survey* 38 (1985): 101–14.

———, ed. *The Second Part of King Henry IV.* The New Cambridge Shakespeare. Cambridge: Cambridge University Press, 1989.

———. *Shakespeare: Politica e contesto economico.* Roma: Bulzoni, 1992.

Mendilow, A. A. "Falstaff's Death of a Sweat." *Shakespeare Quarterly* 9 (1950): 479–83.

Metz, G. Harold, ed. *Sources of Four Plays Ascribed to Shakespeare.* Edited with an Introduction by G. Harold Metz. Columbia: Missouri University Press, 1989.

Morgan, A. E. *Some Problems of Shakespeare's "Henry the Fourth."* London: Shakespeare Association paper, 1924.

Munday, Anthony. *Fedele and Fortunio.* 1585. A Critical Edition by Richard Hosley. New York: Garland, 1981.

Nashe, Thomas. *Pierce Pennilesse his Supplication to the Diuell.* 1592. Facsimile edition. Menston: The Scolar Press, 1969.

Oliver, J. H., ed. *The Merry Wives of Windsor.* New Arden Shakespeare. London: Methuen, 1971.

Painter, William *The Palace of Pleasure.* 1567. Reprint of the 1890 J. Jacobs edition. New York: Dover Publications, 1966.

Prior, Roger. "The Date of *Edward III*." *Notes and Queries* 235 (1990): 178–80.

Prosser, Eleanor. *Shakespeare's Anonymous Editors: Scribe and Compositor in the Folio Text of 2 Henry IV.* Stanford, CA: Stanford University Press 1981.

Proudfoot, Richard. "'The Reign of King Edward III' (1596) and Shakespeare." *Proceedings of the British Academy* 71 (1985): 159–85.

Quiller-Couch, A., and J. Dover Wilson, eds. *The Merry Wives of Windsor.* Cambridge Shakespeare. Cambridge: Cambridge University Press, 1985.

Ribner, Irving. *The English History Play in the Age of Shakespeare.* Princeton: Princeton University Press, 1957.

Roberts, Jeanne Addison. *Shakespeare's English Comedy:* The Merry Wives of Windsor *in Context.* Lincoln: University of Nebraska Press, 1979.

Rossiter, A. P., ed. *Woodstock: A Moral History.* London: Chatto & Windus, 1946.

Salingar, Leo. *Shakespeare and the Traditions of Comedy.* Cambridge: Cambridge University Press, 1974.

Scoufos, Alice-Lyle. "Harvey: A Name Change in *Henry IV*." *Journal of English Literary History* 36 (1961): 297–318.

———. *Shakespeare's Typological Satire: A Study of the Falstaff-Oldcastle Problem.* Athens: Ohio University Press, 1979.

Serpieri, Alessandro. *Otello: L'Eros negato.* Milano: Formichiere, 1978.

Shaaber, Mathias A., ed., *The Second Part of Henry the Fourth.* New Variorum Edition. Philadelphia and London: J. P. Lippincott, 1940.

Simpson, Percy, ed. *The First Part of Sir John Oldcastle,* by Munday, Drayton, Wilson, and Hathaway. 1599. Oxford: Malone Society Reprints, 1908.

———, ed. *Fidele and Fortunio The Two Italian Gentlemen.* Oxford: Malone Society Reprints, 1910.

Slater, Eliot. *The Problem of "The Reign of King Edward III": a Statistical Approach.* Cambridge: Cambridge University Press, 1988.

Smidt, Kristian. *Unconformities in Shakespeare's History Plays.* London: Macmillan, 1982.

Spevack, Marvin, ed. *A Complete and Systematic Concordance to the Works of Shakespeare.* 9 vols. Hildesheim: Georg Olms, 1968–80.

Strathmann, E. A. *Sir Walter Ralegh.* New York: Columbia University Press, 1951.

Strype, John. *Annals of the Reformation.* 6 vols. London, 1725–31.

Tarlton, Richard. *Tarltons Ieasts: drawn into these three parts.* London, 1638.

Taylor, Gary, ed. *Henry V.* Oxford: Oxford University Press, 1983.

———. "The Fortunes of Oldcastle." *Shakespeare Survey* 38 (1985): 85–100.

———. "The Date and Auspices of the Additions to Sir Thomas More." In *Shakespeare and 'Sir Thomas More': Essays on the Play and Its Shakespearean Interest.* Edited by T. H. Howard-Hill, 101–21. Cambridge: Cambridge University Press, 1989.

Tennenhouse, Leonard, *Power on Display: the Politics of Shakespeare's Genres.* London: Methuen, 1986.

Tilley, Morris Palmer. *A Dictionary of the Proverbs in England in the Sixteenth and Seventeenth Centuries.* Ann Arbor: University of Michigan Press, 1950.

Tillyard, E. M. W. *Shakespeare's History Plays.* London: Chatto and Windus, 1944.

Turner, Celeste. *Anthony Mundy: An Elizabethan Man of Letters.* University of California Publications in English, vol. 2, no. 1 (1928).

Vergil, Polydore. *Historia Anglica.* 1555. Facsimile of the 1555 edition. Menston: Scolar Press, 1970.

Weever, John. *The Mirror of Martyrs, or, The life and death of that thrice valiant Captain and most godly Martyr Sir John Oldcastle Knight, Lord Cobham.* 1601. In *The Oldcastle Controversy.* edited by Peter Corbin and Douglas Sedge. Manchester: Manchester University Press, 1991.

Wells, Stanley, and G. Taylor, eds. with John Jowett and William Montgomery. *William Shakespeare: The Complete Works.* Oxford: Clarendon Press, 1986.

Wells, Stanley, and G. Taylor, with John Jowett and William Montgomery. *William Shakespeare: A Textual Companion.* Oxford: Clarendon Press, 1987.

Wiles, David. *Shakespeare's Clown: Actor and Text in the Elizabethan Playhouse.* Cambridge: Cambridge University Press, 1987.

Williams, George Walton. "Fastolf or Falstaff." *English Literary Renaissance* 5 (1975): 308–12.

———. "Second Thoughts on Falstaff's Name." *Shakespeare Quarterly* 30 (1979): 82–84.

Williams, G. Walton, and G. Blakemore Evans, eds. *The History of King Henry the Fourth as Revised by Sir Edward Dering, Bart.* Charlottesville: Folger Facsimiles, 1974.

Willson, Robert F., Jr. "Falstaff in *Henry IV:* What's in a Name?" *Shakespeare Quarterly* 27 (1976): 199–200.

Wilson, John Dover. "The Origins and Development of Shakespeare's 'Henry IV.'" *Library* 4th Series 24 (1945): 2–16.

———, ed. *The Second Part of the History of Henry IV.* Cambridge Shakespeare. Cambridge: Cambridge University Press, 1946.

———. *The Fortunes of Falstaff.* Cambridge: Cambridge University Press, 1953.

Yates, Frances A. *Astraea: The Imperial Theme in the Sixteenth Century.* London: Routledge, 1975.

Yeandle, Laetitia. "The Dating of Sir Edward Dering's copy of 'The History of King Henry the Fourth.'" *Shakespeare Quarterly* 37 (1986): 224–26.

Index

Adams, Douglas, 11
Admiral's men, 23, 70, 89
All's Well That Ends Well, 72, 89
Ariosto, Ludovico, 90: *Orlando Furioso*, 86
Armin, Robert, 71–72, 93, 101, 141n.2
Armstrong, R. L., 144n.28
Axton, Mary, 135n.45

Bale, John, 29, 138n.12
Bandello, Matteo, 122–24, 129
Barton, Anne, 141n.7
Bawcutt, Nigel, 135n.42
Berger, T. L., 139n.15
Berners, John Bourchier, Lord, 120–21, 128, 143n.17
Berry, Philippa, 141n.6, 143n.14
Bevington, David, 24, 133n.3
Bibbiena, Bernardo Dovizi, Cardinal, 90
Boaistuau, Pierre, 123
Boito, Arrigo, 78
Book of Sir Thomas More, The (Munday and others), 13, 24–28, 36, 50, 125, 133nn. 6, 8, 12, 140n.13
Boughner, Daniel, 89, 140nn. 20, 22
Bourchier, Sir Henry, 96, 139n.24
Bradbrook, Muriel C., 13, 127, 144n.33
Brockbank, Philip, 12
Brooke, Henry, eighth Baron Cobham, 106
Brooke, William, seventh Baron Cobham, 32, 98, 100, 102; Brook/Broome change, 101–102
Bullough, Geoffrey, 135n.40

Campbell, Oscar James, 90
Campion, Edmund, 83
Careless Shepherdess, The (Goff), 117
Chamberlain's men, 22, 23, 28–29, 30, 32, 38, 47, 70, 71, 83, 99–101
Chambers, E. K., 141n.14, 142n.17, 143n.7

Chettle, Henry, 23, 133n.6
Clare, Janet, 24, 133n.4
Clubb, Louise, 81, 139–40n.4, 140nn. 8, 15
commedia erudita, 84–86, 87, 89, 90
Conan Doyle, Sir Arthur, 110
Contention between the Houses of Lancaster and York, The (2–3H6), 12, 24
Corbin, Peter, 134nn. 16, 17, 20, 135nn. 35, 1(ch. 2), 139n.18
Coriolanus, 55, 67
Cowl, R. P., 70
Crackstone, Captain (character in *Two Italian Gentlemen*), 84, 86–90; as Falstaff's "ancestor," 88–90
Craik, T. W., 102, 142n.21
Cymbeline, 15, 132

Daniel, Samuel, 54
Davis, Norman, 141n.13
Death of Robert Earl of Huntington, The (Munday and others), 23, 140n.11
Dekker, Thomas, 80, 133n.6
Dennis, John, 79, 141n.5
Dering, Sir Edward, 42, 56, 136n.5
Disobedient Child, The (Ingelend), 138n.11
Doctor Faustus (Marlowe), 24
Doran, Madeleine, 39–40, 135n.47
Downfall of Robert Earl of Huntington, The (Munday and others), 23, 140n.11

Edward II (Marlowe), 117
Edward III, The Reign of King (anonymous), 11, 15, 31, 117–18, 119–29, 132, 143nn. 4, 8, 9, 16; as Garter play, 128–32; authorship, 117–18, 143n.6. *See also* Shakespeare: apocrypha
Edward IV (Heywood), 117
Eliot, Thomas Stearns, 37, 40

151